Critical Guides to French Texts

115 Chateaubriand: Atala *and* R

Critical Guides to French Texts

EDITED BY ROGER LITTLE, WOLFGANG VAN EMDEN, DAVID WILLIAMS

CHATEAUBRIAND

Atala *and* René

Colin Smethurst

Marshall Professor of French
University of Glasgow

Grant & Cutler Ltd
1995

ISBN 0 7293 0384 5

DEPÓSITO LEGAL: V. 29 - 1996

Printed in Spain by
Artes Gráficas Soler, S.A., Valencia
for
GRANT & CUTLER LTD
55-57 GREAT MARLBOROUGH STREET, LONDON W1V 2AY

Contents

Prefatory Note

All quotations from or references to *Atala* and *René* relate to the following edition: Chateaubriand, *Atala. René.* Chronologie et préface par Pierre Reboul, Paris, GF-Flammarion, 1992. This edition, but without the bibliography and chronology of Chateaubriand's life, was first published in 1964 with slightly different pagination. Quotations or references may be located in the earlier edition by adding 3, 4, or 5 pp. to those I give.

The source of all quotations or references may be found in the Select Bibliography at the end of this volume. Thus, '(*6*, p. 10)' refers to the *Essai sur les révolutions...* which is item 6 in the Bibliography. Where no italicized figure starts the reference, item *1*, the edition of the texts specified above, may be assumed.

1. Contexts

(i) *Classical or Romantic? A false problem*

Atala and *René*, two brief narratives, published at the very beginning of the nineteenth century (*Atala* in 1801, *René* in 1802), have generally been seen by literary historians as inaugurating the first generation of French Romanticism. It is true that certain aspects of these early works of Chateaubriand – the focus on the self and luxuriant descriptions of nature – can be found in some eighteenth-century writers such as Jean-Jacques Rousseau and Bernardin de Saint-Pierre; certain eighteenth-century modes of feeling – *sensibilité*, the elegiac – are also echoed by Chateaubriand, but, since he (together with Mme de Staël) has commonly been declared to be a Romantic, such eighteenth-century writings and modes have tended to be called, for literary-historical purposes, pre-Romantic. The latter term has only limited usefulness – what writer ever sat down saying to herself or himself, 'I am going to compose a pre-Romantic work'? – but has produced long-running debates as to the extent to which Chateaubriand still retains such 'pre-Romantic' traits. Other commentators have emphasized the survival of Classical (or neo-Classical or late-Classical) strands of inspiration in Chateaubriand's works. By and large, however, Chateaubriand has been firmly declared to be a Romantic. This often determines a series of stock responses in reading the works, whereby one only picks out those elements which are deemed to be Romantic and underplays or excludes the rest. Thus these two texts have been seen as emphasizing the role of imagination and emotion over that of rationality, promoting a certain image of the individual isolated from fellow humanity and communing only with nature, the whole being underpinned by religious sentiment and a new type of lyrical prose. Such a stereotype has been dinned into the subconscious of generations of hapless French schoolchildren. The figure of René in particular has been used to sum up the myth of the solitary, sick, Romantic soul, suffering from his indefinable *mal du siècle*. The very mention of the title conjures up pictures of doomed love, death, moonlight, exotic natural description, with a tincture of religiosity. The detailed history of the reading of these works over the last 190 years would provide a remarkable insight into French literary education and its role in the French cultural system. These works seem to belong to the very fabric of such a culture. Volume after volume has been filled with arguments over the importance or unimportance of the religious elements in the works or over the religious sincerity or hypocrisy of Chateaubriand himself. Such arguments arise precisely from this French cultural context with its continuing quarrel between the *république laïque* and the Church in French society.

More recently, Pierre Barbéris has reacted fiercely against the earlier stereotype of Romanticism (see *9* and *10*) and has firmly linked Chateaubriand's works, and particularly *René*, with problems of History (with a capital H) and the specific forms of alienation of the individual in modern society. This has been an excellent step forward in underlining a certain sort of realism, defined by Barbéris as figurative expression of the contradictions of evolving social structures. Unfortunately, such a reading seems as partial and as stereotyped as the previously established one. Large sections of Chateaubriand's writings, whole volumes even, are dismissed with remarks like '*Ici Chateaubriand n'écrit pas*'. What is meant here is that, by Barbéris's criteria, Chateaubriand is no longer writing critically and creatively to express the break produced by the French Revolution in the structures of French society. The problem that remains is that there are quite substantial sections in Chateaubriand's publications which are therefore cast into outer darkness as merely stilted academicism or political opportunism. The most famous example of the latter is what Barbéris calls '*l'opération concordataire*'. The concordat of 1802 was a treaty between Napoleon and the Pope, by which the Pope recognized the legitimacy of the Napoleonic régime and in return Napoleon recognized that Catholicism was the religion of the majority of the French nation and guaranteed freedom of worship. This official re-establishment of the Catholic Church after its persecution during the period of the French Revolution was an important factor in securing Napoleon's political position. Thus, Chateaubriand's publication in 1802 of the *Génie du christianisme*, a large work which contained within it the narratives of *Atala* and *René*, and which was designed to prove the superiority of the Christian religion and particularly Catholicism, was undoubtedly an act which could be interpreted as having not only religious but above all political implications. Such an interpretation is doubly reinforced on reading the little-known effusive *Epître dédicatoire au premier consul Bonaparte* published at the head of the 1803 edition of *Génie du christianisme*:

> Citoyen Premier Consul,
> Vous avez bien voulu prendre sous votre protection cette édition du *Génie du Christianisme*; c'est un nouveau témoignage de la faveur que vous accordez à l'auguste cause qui triomphe à l'abri de votre puissance. On ne peut s'empêcher de reconnaître dans vos destinées la main de cette Providence qui vous avait marqué de loin, pour l'accomplissement de ses desseins prodigieux. Les peuples vous regardent; la France, agrandie par vos victoires, a placé en vous son espérance, depuis que vous appuyez sur la Religion les bases de l'Etat et de vos prospérités. Continuez à tendre une main secourable à trente millions de Chrétiens, qui prient pour vous au pied des autels que vous leur avez rendus...

Even allowing for the exaggeration which is customary in the dedicatory genre, this is political boot-licking of a high order. As a result it is impossible to deny a strong element of political opportunism in Chateaubriand's presentation of the pro-religious stand in this work and an attempt to ingratiate himself with the new but powerful Napoleonic State. Chateaubriand was, after all, a recently-returned *émigré* who felt the need to give proof of his reintegration into French public life. Nevertheless to discuss as a consequence, as does Barbéris, all religious elements in Chateaubriand's work as inauthentic or totally ungenuine is clearly an over-statement.

What the traditional literary historians and Barbéris have in common, however, is that they both see Chateaubriand as inaugurating a new type of literature, explicitly or at least implicitly Romantic. What Barbéris has done is to shift the emphasis of what one might mean by Romanticism, firmly attaching it to social and political structures, replacing if you like one stereotype by another.

This volume is not the place to discuss concepts of Romanticism and it may be best simply to note that most definitions nowadays emphasize the diversity of the movement (if movement there be) and pass on. Certainly, there are new elements, new tones, in *Atala* and *René*, but at the same time Chateaubriand was also consciously working within certain generic, thematic and linguistic traditions. Some of these latter one can call Classical – and Chateaubriand explicitly draws attention to them – others belong to themes and modes of discourse seen through an eighteenth-century filter, themes like the noble savage, the good priest, certain concept-ions of the sublime and the picturesque. These may or may not be designated 'Classical' themes. At the least they reflect an eighteenth-century cast of mind. Chateaubriand was, after all, born in 1768 and his formal education was completed well before the French Revolution.

These two apparently simple narratives, then, contain to my mind a whole complex of aims and attitudes which Chateaubriand uses to negotiate for himself a viable if unstable literary, moral and philosophical position. The fragmentariness at moments, the progression by juxtaposition belong to this same quest. Some of the very incoherencies signify unresolved areas of conflict. For this reason I shall be drawing attention to the variety of possible readings of *Atala* and *René*, rather than trying to relate them to the extraneous concepts of Romanticism or Classicism.

(ii) *The interlocking of Chateaubriand's works*

Atala was first published in April 1801, and at that time was
publicly announced by Chateaubriand as forming part of one section
of his forthcoming major work on the nature of Christianity and its
poetic beauty, *Le Génie du christianisme ou les Beautés poétiques
et morales de la religion chrétienne* (pp.29 and 33). The latter was
published in April 1802 with the simplified title *Génie du
christianisme ou beauté de la religion chrétienne*. In the preface to
this first edition, however, he also writes (pp.34-35) that *Atala* was
an episode extracted from the manuscript of another work, an epic
of North American Indians, *Les Natchez*, and that this was part of
the bundle of manuscripts he had composed during his travels to
North America in 1791. *Les Natchez* was finally published in 1826,
though Chateaubriand had clearly rewritten part of it in the
intervening years. From what we know of the dates of composition
of *Les Natchez* and *Le Génie du christianisme*, it is clear that the
earlier inspiration for the work belongs to the Indian epic and that
this was overlaid at a later stage by the study of the poetic beauty of
Christianity. This produces an evident set of tensions in the
narrative.

   That same bundle of manuscripts Chateaubriand claimed to
have brought back from America was also one of the starting points
for the elaborate *Voyage en Amérique*, which was published much
later, in 1827. This work follows the travel genre as it was
understood at the time, with, in addition to the account of
Chateaubriand's own travels, a study of the history and geography
of the continent, a full examination of the way of life of the Indians,
their languages and their modes of government and an assessment
of the present situation of the U.S.A. and the Spanish-American
Republics. It is thus a work which is at one and the same time a
personal memoir (part of it was actually included later in
Chateaubriand's *Mémoires d'outre-tombe*) and a socio-political
study arising from an assessment of the natural and human
environment. It has an air of great erudition but scholars have
shown that in many respects it is largely a work of compilation from

a variety of printed sources. (This was not an unusual mode of composition at the time and modern commentators who talk in terms of plagiarism underestimate the extent to which it was both a well-understood practice and susceptible to creative exploitation. The sacralization of the individual, isolated work is essentially a more recent conception. More or less contemporary with Chateaubriand's creative use of sources is the similar approach adopted by Stendhal in his *Vies de Haydn, Mozart et Métastase* (1815) or his *Vie de Rossini* (1823).) What is interesting for us is the number of cross-references Chateaubriand makes in the *Voyage en Amérique* to *Atala*, for example when he cites the description of the Niagara Falls at the end of *Atala*, or the behaviour of the Indian mother with her dead child. Looking back at *Atala*, therefore, more than 20 years later Chateaubriand sees it, at least in part, as having value for its natural description and its ethnography.

Rather more surprising are the organic links between *Atala* and the first major work of Chateaubriand, the *Essai historique, politique et moral sur les révolutions anciennes et modernes, considérées dans leurs rapports avec la révolution française*, more generally and conveniently known nowadays as the *Essai sur les révolutions* or simply the *Essai*. It was published several years before *Atala*, in 1797. This long, complex and often confusing work is an attempt to understand revolution in general, the French Revolution in particular and, rather more obscurely, Chateaubriand's own relationship to these phenomena. It ends – quite extraordinarily, given the overt subject of the work – with a lyrical evocation of a 'nuit chez les sauvages d'Amérique', describing the fusion of the author with the spirit of the American wilderness. In an attempt to blend this passage with the tone of the political philosopher adopted in the book, he sees the Indians who had offered him hospitality as symbolizing the superiority of the society of natural man over that of civilized man. These elements chime with certain of the aims stated in the preface to the first edition of *Atala* (pp.33 and 36-37), the evocations of American natural scenery and, specifically, the exclamations in the last paragraph of the story.

Thus, the short 70-page narrative of *Atala* can be seen as having links with a veritable constellation of Chateaubriand's major works, each of which itself underwent a number of changes over the years. Many of the fascinating hesitations, ambiguities and obscurities of *Atala* can be seen as the result of this shifting set of relationships between the different works and between their different emphases, socio-political, literary, ethnographic, exotic or personal, and can be explained in terms of them. More importantly, these other works provide possible readings of *Atala*, since Chateaubriand seems not to have made rigid distinctions between different literary genres. For him, the personal recollection, the 'scientific' monograph, the political, religious or philosophical inquiry, the travel book, did not exist in separate compartments. For example, the *Essai sur les révolutions* has the extraordinary opening sentence, 'Qui suis-je? et que viens-je annoncer de nouveau aux hommes?'[1] which might be seen as more appropriate to the narrative of *René* than to a work of political thought. Chateaubriand is perfectly capable of citing the evidence of a scene in the 'literary' work *Atala* to back up a 'scientific' or a religious point. In this he is the direct follower of so many of the eighteenth-century *philosophes* whose philosophical inquiries moved freely back and forth across the range from the scientific to the literary.

To provide, therefore, only a 'literary' study of *Atala* is to deprive it of much of its interest. This leads us to a further problem in analysis: to what extent, even, is it possible to provide a study of only the text of *Atala*, when it is so evident that for Chateaubriand the text overflows its own limits? To take the simplest example, both Chactas and René figure in *Atala, René, Les Natchez, Le Génie du christianisme* and in Chateaubriand's own text or footnote references in *L'Essai sur les révolutions* and *Voyage en Amérique*. For this reason we will try to look at *Atala* and *René* both separately and together, a project encouraged by Chateaubriand himself since already in 1805 he chose to publish the two episodes together in one

---

[1] Possibly a blended reminiscence of the beginning of Jean-Jacques Rousseau's *Rêveries du promeneur solitaire* and his *Confessions*: 'Mais moi, détaché d'eux [from fellow men], que suis-je moi-même?...'

volume. Many modern editions, including the one used here for
reference, continue this pattern.

This interconnecting of Chateaubriand's works is a
phenomenon not unlike the technique used later by Balzac in his
Comédie humaine, where an individual novel may have its own
justification and coherence but also gathers part of its meaning from
its relation to other works. Chateaubriand certainly did not make the
strenuous efforts, as did Balzac, to give a coherent overall structure
to his works, but it is perfectly evident that in a good number of his
writings he is re-working the same basic material. The clearest
example of this is in the *Mémoires d'outre-tombe*. Composed over a
period of some thirty years, they derive part of their interest from
Chateaubriand's own commentaries on re-reading his text.

What we have said so far of *Atala* holds good for the most part
for *René*. There are obviously different emphases: in the latter the
'exotic' American decor is less evident, the problems of the self are
more to the fore – and the narrative creates its own different
demands, but there is still this presence of the figures of Chactas
and René, reference to the Natchez wars and, like a watermark, an
effort to transcribe the effects of the French Revolution on an
individual consciousness.

René was published for the first time in April 1802 as an
episode contained within the *Génie du christianisme*, illustrating
what Chateaubriand called 'le vague des passions'. This context will
provide us with one way of reading *René*. As with *Atala*, however,
the conception of *René* appears to have preceded most of the
composition of the *Génie du christianisme* and many of the
elements in the work sit ill with the proclaimed Christian
apologetics of the *Génie*. The work appeared in several subsequent
editions of the *Génie* and then, as we have said, in 1805
Chateaubriand, claiming he was responding to popular taste,
extracted it and published it jointly with *Atala* to which 'il fait suite
naturelle' (p.56).

Like *Atala*, and a number of Chateaubriand's other
compositions, it is mixed in aim and execution. Again like *Atala*, it

can be seen as belonging to other volumes which effectively constitute a René-Chactas-Amélie-Atala-Céluta cycle of stories, though no simple linearity either of individual psychology or historical events can be deduced from reading them all together. What the other works provide is an enhanced sensitivity to and awareness of what is filtered out, hidden, fudged even, in the relatively sober 'Classical' narratives of *Atala* and *René*.

(iii) *Chateaubriand's 'guides' to reading 'Atala' and 'René'*

Nearly all the modern editions of *Atala* and *René* include the sequence of prefaces Chateaubriand wrote for them. It is perfectly possible to ignore these introductory remarks and go straight to the texts themselves. Giving the prefaces too much weight could well lead to what has been called the 'intentional fallacy', i.e. reading them for the author's intentions and then measuring the extent to which the texts merely exemplify the intentions. Chateaubriand was fully aware of this point: 'Dire ce que j'ai tenté, n'est pas dire ce que j'ai fait' (p.35). Indeed it is rare that there is not some gap, distinction, disruption between an author's intentions and his actual execution and one can even argue that a text which simply carries out faithfully a programme outlined in a preface is not a literary text at all. On the other hand, the prefatory accretions to Chateaubriand's texts have become so much a part of the monumentalization of Chateaubriand's works that it is unrealistic to pretend they are not there, in the name of attempting to achieve a (falsely) naïve reading. They provide a *mise en scène* for the production of the narratives, giving clear – if often conflicting – reasons for them and thus suggest ways of reading the text itself.

Three presentations are particularly worth focusing on: a) the preface to the first edition of *Atala* (1801); b) the context of the *Génie du christianisme*, the work in which *René* was published for the first time (1802) and which incorporated what was effectively the 6th edition of *Atala*; c) the preface to the joint edition of *Atala* and *René* published in 1805.

a) Preface to the first edition of *Atala* (1801)

This preface is preceded by the republication of the letter (p.29) Chateaubriand had had inserted in the *Journal des Débats* and the *Publiciste* a day or two before. Both the letter and the preface proper begin by underlining the fact that *Atala* is an extract from the *Génie du christianisme* which Chateaubriand was to publish a year later and should be seen as forming an integral part of it. Significantly, the full title of the *Génie* is given, presumably to establish it in the reader's mind – a form of pre-publication publicity – but also partly to condition the reader to see in *Atala* a concrete example of 'les beautés poétiques et morales de la religion chrétienne' under the auspices of a new sort of Trinity constituted by the 'harmonies de la religion, avec les scènes de la nature et les passions du cœur humain.' This aesthetic and emotional religion appears to have substituted simply the word Christian for certain forms of deistic faith or natural religion propounded by a number of eighteenth-century French writers, and notably the sense of mysterious harmonies underlying nature and human emotion in Jean-Jacques Rousseau's *Julie ou la nouvelle Héloïse*. It has virtually no theological content and later references to religion in this preface bear out this approach. What Chateaubriand calls the 'calme de la religion' (p.35) seems merely a balancing phrase for the preceding 'calme des déserts'. They are presented as simply two conditioning elements for the essential feature of the book, 'le tableau des troubles de l'amour'. Thus, the three figures of 'harmonies de la religion', 'scènes de la nature' and 'passions du cœur humain' are repeated here, but in reverse order. At the very least, therefore, one can say that no particular priority is accorded the religious over the natural or the passionate. The same process is evident when we look at the literary models Chateaubriand explicitly claims for his work. They are Homer and the Bible, put on an equal footing as 'ces deux grands et éternels modèles du beau et du vrai'. He does not refer to the truth of revealed religion, but to a simple literary truth capable of encapsulating sublime intensity of human emotion. Logically, therefore, he quotes (p.36) the *Iliad* side by side with the Book of

Genesis. Similarly, when Chateaubriand presents (p.37) the figure of the missionary priest, *père* Aubry, the context is at least as much literary as religious. The discussion is produced as part of the presentation of the three main characters. Atala is modestly commended to the reader as 'un caractère assez nouveau'. Her contradictory nature is the result of the Fall of Man, the 'dégradation originelle'. By referring to this merely as an 'antique tradition', however, the direct Biblical reference is avoided or at least underplayed. Chactas is seen as the vehicle for a happy linguistic solution to the problem of making a savage speak in civilized fashion; and *père* Aubry is given as 'le prêtre tel qu'il est', in other words not deformed by Republican prejudice into a 'scélérat fanatique' or by intellectual bias into a mere representative of *philosophe* (presumably deistic) views. For Chateaubriand he is not an extreme figure, but comes as the embodiment of Classical *mesure* or balanced restraint. Chateaubriand is thus playing the Christian card cautiously, for to discuss religion at all was normally seen at the time as implying a political stance. He is seeking above all to avoid being labelled as a party activist or polemicist. Thus it is that in the final reference to religion in the preface (p.38) he subtly shifts the ground. He is not attacking revolutionary fanatics or *philosophes* head-on, nor is he the gallant Christian knight galloping to defend Christianity as the only true faith, but merely the proponent of a fit 'sujet de morale et de littérature'. This is not the language of the evangelist or the zealot. Christianity is, simply, a subject available in the new political climate: 'à présent, sous un gouvernement' qui ne proscrit aucune opinion paisible' (p.38). The contrast is between what Chateaubriand portrays at this stage as the liberalism of the Napoleonic régime and the harshness of the Revolutionary period. It was little more than a year since Napoleon had taken power; Chateaubriand himself had only recently returned from exile in England and was still on the list of *émigré* aristocrats and so technically in the country illegally. Political flattery of Napoleon as the man sent by Providence 'en signe de réconciliation' (p.34) and the man permitting a favourable presentation of Christianity is understandable in the circumstances. Such flattery was to become even more obvious with the publication of the *Génie du christianisme* a year later. Evidence such as this has often been adduced to demonstrate Chateaubriand's religious hypocrisy. For the moment, all we need do is underline the fact that there is a political context in which the Christian 'sujet de morale et de littérature' is functioning.

It seems very likely, too, that politics in the form of French colonial policy is one of the factors behind the choice of the Natchez and the Louisiana setting as a starting-point for the work. Chateaubriand says 'je ne vis pas de sujet plus intéressant, surtout pour des Français...' (p.33). Originally a French colony, Louisiana, its very name the result of homage to Louis XIV, passed to Spain as one of the results of the Treaty of Paris (1763) which had ended the Seven Years War, but was restored to France in 1800 by the secret accord of San Ildefonso. Sovereignty was only temporary, for Napoleon sold it to the U.S. Government in 1803.[2] The date of publication of *Atala* thus sets it in that sort of period of time when the colony was nominally returned to French control. Chateaubriand could feel that an important step had been taken in recovering the former French possessions in North America. This goes some way to explaining the colonial nostalgia expressed later in the opening words of the prologue. The interest in the search for the North-West passage (pp.33-34), which could have led to discoveries 'utiles à mon pays' (p.34), also speaks of nostalgia for the lost territories of Nouvelle-France or Canada. Chateaubriand returns to this theme of lost colonies in the last paragraph of the preface. The juxtaposition of the deep South (Louisiana, p.33) and the Canadian North (pp.33 and 39) hints at the construction of an America in Chateaubriand's mind and consequently in *Atala* which is a mixture of observed reality, political dreaming and fictional necessity.

This conflation of the two extremes of the North American continent can be paralleled by what appears in the preface as an incoherent view of natural man. What constitutes man in the state of

---

[2] One wonders why successive readings of *Atala* in France never link it to that major event in U.S. history generally referred to as the Louisiana purchase. Even Barbéris's political reading ignores the point.

nature and the relative virtues and vices of nature and civilization
had been one of the major focuses of intellectual debate ever since
the latter part of the seventeenth century. Most recently, the major
contribution had been in the works of Jean-Jacques Rousseau, whom
Chateaubriand cites (p.36) as 'un enthousiaste des Sauvages'.
Alluding to the famous statement in Rousseau's *Discours sur
l'origine de l'inégalité*: 'que l'homme qui médite est un animal
dépravé', Chateaubriand comes down firmly on the opposite side
and in support of 'thought' and 'civilization', joining hands thereby
with a number of the *philosophes* of the earlier part of the
eighteenth century. Then, by linguistic sleight of hand, he switches
from one sense of 'nature' to another in order to condemn bourgeois
realism and drama, in the name of Classical perfection and ideal
canons of beauty: 'Peignons la nature, mais la belle nature...' It is
hardly possible to find a clearer statement of Classical literary
idealism. This preference for 'civilized' man is, of course, in total
opposition to his opening statement in the Preface where he says he
aimed to write the epic of natural man, seen as embodying notions
of freedom and justice. These opposing aims undoubtedly represent
two different stages in Chateaubriand's reactions to the topos of
nature versus civilization. From what we know of the history of the
composition of *Atala*, it is evident that at an early phase in its
conception Chateaubriand adopted what was broadly a Rousseauist
attitude, seeing natural man as innocent. At a later stage, a desire
for order and stability is conveniently formulated in neo-Classical
(and hence anti-Rousseau) terms. Thus, in the space of four pages,
we have two statements which are logically incompatible. This sort
of literal incoherence is quite common in Chateaubriand's work and
seems to me to be best seen as an early symptom of Chateaubriand's
striving for a political synthesis between freedom and order,
individual liberty and traditional authority. Clearly, this Preface
comes nowhere near such a synthesis, but it does at least put down
markers indicating the boundaries between which both
Chateaubriand's political thinking and his literary expression will
function. Because the aim is so vast, the boundaries so wide-set, he
left himself very open to criticism. Politically, he came at a later

stage to be seen as an exponent of an eccentric form of liberalism which sat awkwardly with his own conception of divine-right, legitimate monarchism, and ended as suspect to both liberals and legitimists. In an early work like *Atala*, one can see him beginning to negotiate a position viable and satisfactory at least to himself on the basis of his reading and his personal experience.

In terms of the literary form of the work and the discussions of characters, the main thrust of the Preface is an attempt at a classicizing tone. Not only does Chateaubriand refer to Homer as a source of inspiration, he also points to the Classical simplicity of structure, with prologue, *récit* and epilogue. The whole approach adopted in order to speak of his literary aims (pp.35-38) is remarkably similar to the tone of, say, Corneille's *Discours* on his plays. The aim is to 'rappeler la littérature à ce goût antique, trop oublié de nos jours' (p.38). Such a position may seem quite remarkable when we know the way in which literary historians have so firmly linked Chateaubriand to the new Romantic movement. Basically, however, it seems a stand against revolutionary excess and the more melodramatic representations of emotion promoted in the name of extremer forms of eighteenth-century *sensibilité*. Such a stand does not prevent the smuggling into his own work of new features, features which may themselves have more in common than Chateaubriand cares to admit with *sensibilité* and excess or even frenzy. It does serve to point, however, to the extent to which the Classicizing spirit, as late as 1801, can be seen as the vehicle for renewal and rejuvenation of literature. At the beginning of the nineteenth century the Classical standpoint was not just the dead end of an exhausted tradition, as it is so often portrayed. Within the Classical tradition, however, one notes a certain shift of emphasis from Rome to Greece, and the references to Homer often serve to underline the Homeric as the epic of 'primitive', 'natural' man. Just such a positive approach to the Classical spirit is found intermittently in André Chénier's poem *L'Invention* (1783-90), where he calls for modern scientific advance and human experience to be expressed in a literary form worthy of comparison with the perfection of the art of Antiquity, summed up in his famous:

> Sur des pensers nouveaux faisons des vers antiques.[3]

Interestingly, Chénier's poem was to have been a sort of preface to what he hoped to achieve in two large-scale works, *Hermès* and *L'Amérique*, which together were intended to be an epic of nature, man and all types of human society. One can thus see the epic treatment and the American theme indissolubly linked in the mind of the two authors. Where the two part company, however, is in the fact that Chénier's modern epic spirit led him to put more weight on scientific and philosophical progress, whereas Chateaubriand's experience of the French Revolutionary period impelled him to put more stress on the impasse at the human level into which simpler notions of progress had led humanity.

This relatively long examination of the Preface to the first edition of *Atala* hardly exhausts its interest. One could also cite literary politics with the Fontanes-Mme de Staël affair (pp.38-39 and the footnote to p.35) or the incorporation of personal experience in the bitter recollection of the fate of members of his family during the Revolutionary period (p.34 and footnote). But enough has been said perhaps to underline the complexity, the as yet unresolved notions and, occasionally, the woolliness or confusion of purpose of this brief preface.

b) The *Génie du christianisme*

When we turn to the presentation of *Atala* and *René* in the context of the *Génie du christianisme* we can see a much firmer effort at providing a single voice or a single reading of the texts. Firstly, the context itself almost dwarfs the two narratives, which provide about one eighth of the work as a whole. Against this, it must be said that *Atala* and *René* are by far the longest 'chapters' in the work. With the exception of the final chapter of the *Génie*, which has seventeen pages, no chapter exceeds ten pages and most are only two or three pages long. *Atala* and *René* are thus in that sense unusual and outstanding elements.

---

[3] Chénier, *L'Invention*, line 184.

The overall structure of the *Génie* gives an appearance of great solidity. The work is divided into four parts: I – *Dogmes et doctrine*, II – *Poétique du christianisme*, III – *Beaux-Arts et littérature*, and IV – *Culte*. Parts I and IV are each divided into six Books and Parts II and III into five Books (though originally each Part was to have had six Books). Each Book is further subdivided into a variable number of chapters. The opening and closing Parts of the work are mainly concerned with the theology and practice of religion; Parts II and III seem from the titles the literary meat in the religious sandwich. Within this very broad distinction the picture in detail is rather more blurred. Nevertheless, the general impression is conveyed of a strong doctrinal framing for the two 'literary' parts. As we might expect, *René* and *Atala* are to be found in the 'literary' sections, *René* about the middle of Part II, and *Atala* at the very end of Part III. So far, in referring to the two texts, we have placed *Atala* before *René*, simply because *Atala* was published first. Here the order is reversed. What has happened is that the structure of the *Génie* has determined the position of the two texts to the detriment of any historical verisimilitude. Not only was *Atala* published first, but historically the events of *Atala* take place well before those of *René*, and, according to the text, Chactas's narrative was recounted before René's. In the *Génie du christianisme*, however, the literary-religious thesis takes priority.

This thesis is stated in the introductory chapter to the work. Its aim is to counter the multiplicity of attacks on Christianity throughout the ages, to demolish what Chateaubriand implies is the consensus arrived at by the end of the eighteenth century, namely that 'le christianisme n'était qu'un système barbare dont la chute ne pouvait arriver trop tôt pour la liberté des hommes, le progrès des lumières, les douceurs de la vie, et l'élégance des arts' (6, p.468). Chateaubriand works to reverse every one of these criteria, not by theological argument or detailed discussion of dogma, but by trying to show that 'de toutes les religions qui ont jamais existé la religion Chrétienne est la plus poétique, la plus humaine, la plus favorable à la liberté, aux arts et aux lettres... il fallait appeler tous les enchantements de l'imagination, et tous les intérêts du cœur au secours de cette... religion' (*6*, pp.469-70). The Christian religion 'se prête merveilleusement aux élans de l'âme, et peut enchanter l'esprit aussi divinement que les dieux de Virgile et d'Homère' (*6*, p.470). Among a vast quantity of historical, literary and human examples, what Chateaubriand calls his two 'anecdotes' find their place. They are simply two 'tableaux' (*6*, p.471) to be admired. And if problems of faith concerning the existence of God raise their ugly head, the response is simply 'nous cherchons seulement nos preuves dans les merveilles de la nature... nous essayons de frapper au cœur de l'incrédule de toutes les manières' (*6*, pp.471-72).

The strategic aim of the second and third Parts of the *Génie* is to show how Christianity has inspired works of art throughout the centuries which are equal or in many cases superior to the finest works of (pagan) Antiquity. Given the practically universal recognition in Europe at that time of the primacy of the Classical world in this domain, Chateaubriand is measuring works imbued with the Christian spirit by the highest possible standards. Thus, in Part II, Book 1, in accordance with Classical criteria, Chateaubriand begins by discussing epic poetry. Homer and Virgil are compared with Dante, Tasso, Milton. Voltaire's *Henriade*, writes Chateaubriand, might have figured in this pantheon, were it not for his lack of religious feelings.

In Book 2, Chateaubriand goes on to discuss the importance of religion in the creation of literary figures which he calls natural characters, such as the married couple (here he compares and contrasts Homer's Ulysses and Penelope with Milton's Adam and Eve), the father, the mother, the son, the daughter, in order to arrive at the conclusion that 'le christianisme n'enlève rien au poète des caractères *naturels*, tels que pouvait les représenter l'antiquité, et il lui offre de plus son *influence* sur ces mêmes caractères. Il augmente donc nécessairement la *puissance*, puisqu'il augmente le *moyen*, et multiplie les *beautés* dramatiques, en multipliant les *sources* dont elles émanent' (*6*, p.672). A strong, if abstract and ultimately rather misty, statement of principle.

This simple 'ideological' point of view is, however, largely undermined when he goes on to discuss the first of what he calls

'caractères sociaux', that of the priest. Having briefly referred the
reader to the fourth Part of the *Génie*, where he is to examine
various types of priest, he then proceeds to compare Virgil and
Racine, a comparison which appears to fascinate him. Although
Racine's *Athalie* is described as 'l'œuvre le plus parfait du génie
inspiré par la religion' (6, p.677), a point fully consonant with the
strategy of the *Génie*, Chateaubriand's characterization of Virgil's
poetry is nevertheless much more sympathetically done. The
ideological 'cause' at this point – the superiority of the Christian
priest in literature – is completely overridden for the time being by
an evocation whose links with Chateaubriand himself and with
René are quite startling. Compared with Racine's , Virgil's 'voix ...
est plus gémissante et sa lyre plus plaintive' (6, p.677). This is seen
as an excellent feature in Virgil; Racine would have been capable of
achieving this, but 'il vécut trop à la ville, pas assez dans la
solitude', his works are too redolent of the Court and Versailles.
The cause of Virgil's sense of melancholy, however, was 'le
sentiment des malheurs qu'il éprouva dans sa jeunesse. Chassé du
toit paternel, il garda toujours le souvenir de sa Mantoue... Virgile
cultiva ce germe de tristesse en vivant seul au milieu des bois...
Ainsi, des chagrins de famille, le goût des champs, un amour-propre
en souffrance, et des passions non satisfaites, s'unirent pour lui
donner cette rêverie qui nous charme dans ses écrits.' In other
words, at this point in the *Génie*, Virgil prefigures Chateaubriand's
literary persona and his creature René. The following chapter, in
which Chateaubriand compares warrior figures in the form of the
hero of Antiquity as against the knight of chivalry and finds for the
superiority of the latter, simply reverts without transition to the
dominant thesis of the *Génie*. We shall find similar jump cuts when
we come to look more closely at the texts of *Atala* and *René*. It is as
if a curtain is briefly lifted to reveal an alternative mental décor, one
which has either more intimate links with the personality of the
individual than with the 'public' problems of religious politics or
else provides us with an alternative hidden interpretation of the
'public' thesis. We have already noted the strong Classicizing
instincts of much of Chateaubriand's thought and it is reasonable to

link Chateaubriand's conception of Classical restraint with this half-revelation of an alternative agenda and an alternative way of seeing the world. We know already from the Preface to the first edition of *Atala* that he chooses to portray an idealized version of reality, 'la belle nature'. The two concluding chapters of Part II, Book 2, of the *Génie*, which follow on immediately from the Virgil-Racine chapter, are significantly focused on a definition of 'le beau idéal', seen as 'l'art *de choisir et de cacher*'.[4] This art, profoundly Classical in its origins, is one of the keys to understanding our two texts.

1) '*René*' in the '*Génie du christianisme*'

In Part II, Book 3 (i.e. the book which in the original editions of the *Génie* immediately precedes *René*) Chateaubriand moves from comparisons between Classical and Christian portrayals of what he calls characters (mainly social relations or functions) to comparisons between the respective portrayals of passions. Chateaubriand says – and it is a measure of how far he has moved from points of doctrine or theology – that a major advantage of Christianity is that it gives rise to a superior type of literature because it puts a brake on human passions and thereby increases the sense of conflict, and it is precisely on such conflicts that literature thrives: 'la religion chrétienne est un vent céleste qui enfle les voiles de la vertu, et multiplie les orages de la conscience autour du vice' (*6*, p.686). The presence of this divine afflatus means that not only is Racine's Phèdre more passionate than Virgil's Dido, but also, because she is in Chateaubriand's eyes a Christian wife, the sense of horror aroused by her incestuous love is increased: 'L'inceste n'était pas une chose si rare et si monstrueuse chez les anciens, pour exciter de pareilles frayeurs dans le cœur du coupable' (*6*, p.692). Both *René* and *Atala* are narratives which recount an incestuous or quasi-incestuous love. Commentaries on this aspect of the two texts

---

[4] *6*, p.681. This section of the *Génie* on the *beau idéal* repeats with variations the content of a famous letter of Chateaubriand's to Fontanes dated 22 December 1800.

usually flutter around Chateaubriand's relationship with his sister
Lucile and pose the question whether their love for each other went
beyond normal sibling love or not. Chateaubriand's discretion has
ensured that the matter remains unresolved. The text we have just
quoted, however, raises the more interesting possibility that the
theme of incestuous love, consecrated by his beloved Classical
authors, but augmented in intensity by the presence of Christian
faith, may have been determined in his mind because it was a
particularly strong topos which allowed him to increase the sense of
conflict, the Christian values, and, to his mind, the *literary* virtues
of his texts.

Further chapters in Part II, Book 3 of the *Génie* provide extra
examples of the literary superiority of the portrayal of Christian
passion, showing at the same time the variety of types of Christian
love. Thus, the terrifying passion of Phèdre becomes in the portrait
of Jean-Jacques Rousseau's Julie (in *Julie, ou la nouvelle Héloïse*)
'de mélodieux soupirs: c'est une voix troublée, qui sort d'un
sanctuaire de paix, un cri d'amour que prolonge, en l'adoucissant,
l'écho religieux des tabernacles' (*6*, p.694). This Rousseauist blend
of love and religion has, in addition, the literary virtue of creating a
new type of tenderness, and as a result a 'nouveau langage des
passions'. Further examples are Richardson's Clementina in
Charles Grandison, Heloïse in Pope's *Heloïse to Abeilard*, and
Virginie in Bernardin de Saint-Pierre's *Paul et Virginie*.

This sequence of titles and authors provides in part an outline
guide to eighteenth-century *sensibilité* and, implicitly, an indication
of some of the literary models and justifications for *René*. It is as
though each of the examples contributes a piece to the overall
picture of love of René and Amélie. Indeed, so many of the
examples are those of feminine suffering that one almost expects
them to determine a work called *Amélie* rather than *René*. This
transfer of what was seen at the time as 'feminine' sensibility to the
male figure of René is worth noting as part of Chateaubriand's
feminization of male desire. I have already mentioned the incest
theme deriving from the example of Phèdre. Pope's work, on the
other hand, is praised for the fine, dramatic opposition it provides

between 'les chagrins et l'amour d'Héloïse, et le calme et la chasteté de la vie religieuse' (*6*, p.700), precisely the choice offered to Amélie.

The example of *Paul et Virginie* and its influence on Chateaubriand has been alluded to by many critics. Here, however, I would underline its presence in the chapters of the *Génie* immediately preceding *René* as providing the reader with a sort of conditioning to accept the tone and type of narrative that is about to be produced. *Paul et Virginie* had been a prodigious popular success since its publication in 1788. Chateaubriand stresses 'une certaine morale mélancolique qui brille dans l'ouvrage' (*6*, p.705), notes particularly the simplicity of the *récit* and, as a prefiguring of his own *récit* which follows ten or so pages further on, picks out the fact that it was included in Bernardin de Saint-Pierre's *Etudes de la nature* in order to 'justifier les voies de Dieu, et... prouver les beautés de la religion' (*6*, p.706), in other words, precisely the programme of the *Génie* and the function of *René* (and later *Atala*) within it. Even the dramatic catastrophe of *Paul et Virginie* is analysed in such a way that it sounds virtually identical to the dramatic crisis in *Atala*, when Atala poisons herself in order to remain faithful to her vow of eternal virginity. It purports to demonstrate, too, the same 'ideological' function. When the ship which is bringing her back to her virtuous lover is wrecked just off-shore, Virginie refuses steadfastly to strip off her clothes and swim to safety. For Chateaubriand, 'Virginie meurt pour conserver une des premières vertus recommandées par l'Evangile. Il eut été absurde de faire mourir une Grecque [i.e. a representative of pagan Antiquity], pour ne vouloir pas dépouiller ses vêtements. Mais l'amante de Paul est une vierge *chrétienne*, et le dénouement, ridicule sous une croyance moins pure, devient ici sublime' (*6*, p.706). At first reading modern sensibilities find the dramatic crisis in both *Atala* and *Paul et Virginie* ridiculous, and a deeply unconvincing demonstration of the superiority of Christian inspiration in literature. This is an area in which public taste has shifted immeasurably since the end of the eighteenth century. Such scenes are only credible and moving nowadays if read with a sympathetic understanding of the aims and techniques of eighteenth-century *sensibilité* (see pp.51-53 below).

2) *Du vague des passions*

The last chapter of Part II, book 3 of the *Génie*, and the one that finally introduces *René*, is the famous and much-quoted one titled 'Du vague des passions'. This chapter is reproduced (pp.56-58) in the edition of *Atala* and *René* which we are using as a basic reference, but in a way which distorts significantly its importance for an understanding of how *René* was presented to the readers of the *Génie du christianisme* in 1802.[5]

What is the argument of this celebrated chapter? Antiquity, says Chateaubriand, was largely concerned with the 'here-and-now' of politics and physical well-being (p.57) and did not, as Christians must, measure everyday existence against the life everlasting, against eternity. Furthermore, most of Chateaubriand's examples, as we have seen, concern female figures. Thus, it is perfectly logical for him to propose an extension of his argument to a male figure, in order to demonstrate that the literary superiority of the presence of Christian faith is available in the portrait of both sexes. He is careful, however, to indicate that in modern society the greater role and influence of women ('Les femmes, chez les peuples modernes...', p.57) have helped to create such a figure, have made men, particularly young men, more susceptible to the dramatic stresses produced by Christian faith:[6]

---

[5] Although the GF-Flammarion edition (*1*) calls the Preface in which it appears 'Préface de 1805', it contains large pieces which were present in some but not all of the editions of the *Génie du christianisme* from 1802 on, but which were in fact *suppressed* in the Preface to the joint publication of *Atala* and *René* in 1805. For example, from 'Enfin, les Grecs et les Romains' to 'dans un cœur solitaire'. Also 'Ce n'est pour ainsi dire' to 'dans l'histoire de René'. Thus, in its essentials the GF-Flammarion text (pp.56-58) is that of the 1802 or 1803 editions of the *Génie du christianisme*.

[6] This is probably a reflection of Mme de Staël's view in *De la littérature* (1800) of the increased role of women in the modern world. Chateaubriand,

nos passions [i.e. those of men, as opposed to women],
amollies par le mélange des leurs [i.e. those of women],
prennent à la fois quelque chose d'incertain et de tendre.
(p.57)

The crucial point is that this uncertainty and tenderness, *in the
context of the Génie*, is a positive *virtue*. It is a new and richer form
of emotion, produced by the presence of the Christian faith, and one
that was not available to the writers of Antiquity, because their
religion gave them no conception of the pleasures of life after death
to set against the tribulations of life on earth. They were, therefore,
not susceptible to the charms of *rêverie* (again, in this context, a
positive term):

> ...les Grecs et les Romains, n'étendant guère leurs
> regards au-delà de la vie, et ne soupçonnant point des
> plaisirs plus parfaits que ceux de ce monde, n'étaient
> point portés, comme nous, aux rêveries et au désirs par
> le caractère de leur religion. C'est dans le génie du
> Christianisme qu'il faut surtout chercher la raison de ce
> *vague* des sentiments répandu chez les hommes
> modernes. (p. 57)

The impact of this last sentence is truly extraordinary, when one
considers that most commentators, and Chateaubriand himself
indeed at a later stage, present this 'vague des passions' [7] as deeply

---

here as throughout the *Génie*, is working against a very broad historical
backcloth of human history: expressions like 'chez les peuples modernes'
and 'chez les hommes modernes' have to be seen against expressions
like 'Les Anciens', 'les Grecs et les Romains'. The turning-point, in
Chateaubriand's historical perception, between the Ancient and Modern is
'l'invasion des Barbares' (p.58). Within the context of the *Génie*, therefore,
it is abusive to interpret, as does Barbéris, references to modern life as
meaning unambiguously Regency, post-revolutionary, Napoleonic or
bourgeois France.

[7] N.B. '*le* vague des passions', i.e. all that is indeterminate, not fixed on a
concrete object, in human emotions.

harmful to the human psyche. Within the context of the *Génie du christianisme*, and certainly as it was first presented to the public, *René* was a moral tale, a positive example of the literary superiority of Christian – as opposed to Classical – inspiration, a living case of the experience of the emptiness of existence set against the fullness of a Christian conception of the universe. In the argument of the *Génie du christianisme*, therefore, René does not, as is often said, wallow in self-pity; rather he derives positive pleasure from contemplating present misery as, implicitly, a guarantee of happiness after death.

It is only at a later stage that a hidden incoherence is reinforced and that the simple, consistent argument of the *Génie* is substantially undermined. The evocation in the first paragraph of the chapter 'Du vague des passions' ('Il reste à parler...désabusé de tout', p.56) is at one and the same time consonant with the general argument – it fits into the broad historical sweep of the chapter and of the *Génie* ('Plus les peuples avancent en civilisation...'), but in its characterization of the nature of youthful imagination the reader is also confusingly encouraged to think in terms of the 'youth of today' ('le grand nombre d'exemples qu'on a sous les yeux'). Just as with the role of women in modern society, one asks oneself if Chateaubriand is referring, say, to the role of women in mediaeval chivalrous society and the growth of *courtoisie* or much more specifically to the social and intellectual role of women in the late eighteenth century. Both these examples, however, are kept in the first edition of the *Génie* at the level of possible interpretations, hinted ambiguities. Just the same confusion arises because the original chapter of the *Génie* ended as follows:

> c'est la peinture du *vague des passions*, sans aucun mélange d'aventures, hors un malheur, qui, sans produire d'événements remarquables, sert seulement à redoubler la mélancolie de René et à le punir. On trouvera d'ailleurs dans cet épisode quelques harmonies des monuments Chrétiens et de la vie religieuse, avec

les passions du cœur et les tableaux de la nature: ainsi
notre but sera doublement rempli.

It is only in later editions that Chateaubriand adds part of a
sentence, to make explicit the contemporary significance of René
and to underline the extent to which he condemns his behaviour. At
the same time he clarifies the nature of the double aim of the *Génie*
(see bottom p.58). The crucial addition is: 'et pour effrayer les
jeunes hommes qui, livrés à d'inutiles rêveries, se dérobent
criminellement aux charges de la societé.'

We now have a René who is morally condemned as socially
irresponsible and a warning to the youth of today. This point of view
is of course at odds with the original aim of the *René* anecdote in
the *Génie* and is an example of one of the apparent incoherences of
presentation. What may have been in Chateaubriand's mind is that,
between the first and the second editions, reader response and
Chateaubriand's own relationship with the Napoleonic régime had
shown up the potentially deleterious effect of a certain reading of
René (and, to a lesser extent, *Atala*) if full regard were not paid to
the overall shape of the *Génie*. Rather than urging his readers to re-
read all the *Génie*, Chateaubriand prefers to simplify his moral line
in relation to the René figure, and it is this which introduces the
seeming incoherence. In any case, readers were already pressing
Chateaubriand to separate *René* and *Atala* from the body of the
Génie. Even today, however, it is possible to salvage some
coherence, as the Mark Two version of René is condemned for
'inutiles rêveries', which leaves open the possibility of 'utiles
rêveries', i.e. those directed toward thoughts of God and in harmony
with Christian institutions. René's meditations are not so directed,
and therefore pointless, indeed harmful.

3) *Atala* in the *Génie du christianisme*

Curiously, *Atala* appears much less integrated into the argument of
the *Génie* than does *René*; curiously, because, as we have seen,
Atala contributed part of the pre-publicity for the *Génie* and was

firmly announced as forming an integral part of the work. The chapters preceding *Atala* are much as announced in the letter Chateaubriand published in 1801 (p.29), but compared with the initially relatively clear logic surrounding the presentation of *René*, *Atala* completes a Part III which, while starting just as systematically, ends more obscurely.

Within the general remit of *Beaux-Arts et littérature*, Book 1 is devoted to music, painting, sculpture and architecture, all dealt with in summary fashion; Book 2, entitled *Philosophie*, covers science, philosophy and certain *moralistes*; Book 3 deals with the art of the historian, and Book 4 with the art of oratory (*Eloquence*). What we can see here is a traditional conception of the division of knowledge and rhetoric expounded in the service of Christianity. Book 4 ends with a crucial chapter, a lament that the lack of Christian faith displayed by most of the writers of the eighteenth century has produced a literature inferior to that of the seventeenth century. The whole chapter is intended as an illustration of the proposition 'Que l'incrédulité est la principale cause de la décadence du goût et du génie':

> Un écrivain qui refuse de croire en un Dieu auteur de l'univers, et juge des hommes dont il a fait l'âme immortelle bannit d'abord l'infini de ses ouvrages...Il ne voit rien de noble dans la nature...Si l'incrédule se trouve ainsi borné dans les choses de la nature, comment peindra-t-il l'homme avec éloquence? Les mots pour lui manquent de richesse...sans religion, *point de sensibilité.*' (*6*, pp.867 and 869, Chateaubriand's emphasis)

Thus it is that Book 5 is intended implicitly to suggest topics to remedy this deplorable state of literary taste created, as Chateaubriand sees it, by the atheism of the eighteenth century. This is the book referred to in his prefatory letter to *Atala* as *Harmonies de la religion...* (p.29). In the *Génie* it is called 'Harmonies de la religion *chrétienne* avec les scènes de la nature et les passions du cœur humain'. Just as with the earlier argument concerning the passions which introduced *René*, so here the principle is that the presence of Christian faith reinfuses life into descriptions of natural scenery and human emotions which otherwise would be meaningless, mere ashes, dust. In fact, the chapters of the book meander back and forth between the siting of monasteries in the desert, the poetry of ruins, certain artistic conceptions of the picturesque ('Les ruines, considérées sous les rapports du paysage, sont plus pittoresques dans un tableau, que le monument frais et entier', *6*, p.883), and popular religious practices which establish links between natural environment and religious faith ('Il ne s'agit pas d'examiner rigoureusement ces croyances...Il s'agit seulement de savoir si leur but est moral, si elles tendent mieux que les lois elles-mêmes à conduire la foule à la vertu', *6*, p.891).

It is this obscure attempt to offer a number of fit Christian literary subjects which leads directly to Book 6, that is the story of *Atala*, presented as an attempt to link together or fuse the suggested subjects scattered through the chapters of Book 5: 'Nous allons maintenant confondre les harmonies précédentes... Mais au lieu de donner des préceptes, nous offrirons des exemples; l'auteur se taira pour laisser parler d'autres personnages' (*6*, p.1831).

Thus, *Atala* not only completes the 'literary' section of the *Génie*, it also has the crucial creative function of attempting to roll back the harmful effects of the literature of the eighteenth century.

The fourth and final part of the *Génie* in principle is no longer concerned with matters literary, but with aspects of Christian devotion. In practice, as always with Chateaubriand, divisions which appear rigid are in fact extremely flexible. Just as Chateaubriand's works interlock, so within this work the sections interpenetrate. In the fourth part of the *Génie*, for example, Chateaubriand devotes a whole book to missionary activities, in the course of which he evokes an encounter (real? imagined?) with a missionary priest who resembles in many respects the *père* Aubry figure in *Atala* (*6*, pp.1005-06). Conversely, the 'literary' or 'creative' work *Atala* (like *René*) contains many of the aesthetic, religious, political and personal preoccupations evident elsewhere in the *Génie* and in Chateaubriand's works in general.

c) The Joint Preface to *Atala* and *René* (1805)

I have already referred to the preface of 1805 which in the GF-Flammarion edition is called unfortunately 'Preface d'*Atala*'. It is in fact the preface to the joint edition of both *Atala* and *René* and should be read as such. I have also indicated that two passages which were present in the *Génie du christianisme* chapter on the *vague des passions* were cut out of this 1805 preface.

This new presentation of the two works, here published side by side for the first time, but now separated from the rest of the *Génie du christianisme*, shows us a Chateaubriand extremely aware of the public, or range of publics, for which he intended his work. He refers first to an abridgement of the *Génie* he had permitted for educational purposes. This abridgement had eliminated both *Atala* and *René*, together with a good part of the 'poétique du christianisme' as unsuitable for the eyes of the young. *Atala* and *René* are described as 'uniquement destinée[s] aux gens du monde' (p.51). It is not clear whether the 'autre classe de lecteurs' a few lines further on refers to the 'gens du monde', who required, according to Chateaubriand, to have the apologetics of the *Génie* sweetened by the two anecdotes, or whether a third class of reader is intended, a readership totally uninterested in all the Christian apparatus. Maybe Chateaubriand saw them as two overlapping audiences. The best insight into the 'gens du monde' readership is offered by Chateaubriand himself in the course of the pamphlet he published in May 1803, called *Défense du Génie du christianisme*, in which he says that you have to talk to readers in terms they understand. You can write endless weighty volumes of theology but they will only be read by specialists or by committed Christians. If you really wish to roll back all the standard assumptions of the general book-reading public, then you have to use attractive techniques: 'commencez par vous faire lire. Ce dont vous avez besoin d'abord, c'est un ouvrage religieux qui soit pour ainsi dire populaire' (*6*, p.1099). 'Populaire' in this case has of course none of the sense of 'peuple' contained in it, but everything to do with being pleasing. Chateaubriand urges: 'Persuadez à la jeunesse qu'un honnête homme peut être chrétien sans être un sot...' This 'jeunesse' is not the schoolchildren for whom the abridgement was made, but rather leisured young adults, specifically young men, young writers or those interested in literature (both the latter seem implied in Chateaubriand's use of the expression *gens de lettres*) and those who set the tone in society. The work is written 'surtout pour les *gens de lettres* et pour le *monde*... Si l'on ne part point de cette base, que l'on feigne toujours de méconnaître la classe de lecteurs à qui le *Génie du christianisme* est particulièrement adressé, il est assez clair qu'on ne doit rien comprendre à l'ouvrage. Cet ouvrage a été fait pour être lu de l'homme de lettres le plus incrédule, du jeune homme le plus léger, avec la même facilité que le premier feuillette un livre impie, le second un roman dangereux' (*6*, pp.1099-1100). Just as Voltaire had employed his talents to make lack of piety socially acceptable, so Chateaubriand writes to use his to make religion acceptable, agreeable, fashionable even. Why should the devil have all the best tunes?

This awareness of audience and of the social and, as we will see later, political implications of his writing provides a conditioning for the reading of the text which, whatever one's interpretation or interpretations, cannot be naïve or innocent. The portrait, say, of the solitary 'moi' in *René* is not idle literary fancy.

Two further points arise from the remainder of this 1805 preface. The first is that it demonstrates one of the constant literary techniques of Chateaubriand, which is to salvage and recycle earlier texts, effectively quoting himself, then using the texts as springboards for further commentary, thereby giving a depth of perspective to his work. Thus here he recycles, with the changes of emphasis we have noted, the chapter from the *Génie du christianisme* on the *vague des passions* and also an extract from the *Défense du Génie du christianisme*.[8]

---

[8] The apotheosis of this technique is to be found in the *Mémoires d'outre-tombe*, in which there is a constant to-ing and fro-ing between the period of

Secondly, he is concerned to answer literary objections to his texts, but mainly to respond to moral or religious scruples on the part of his critics. The section concerned with *René* insists particularly on the novelty of the subject and relates it (p.60) to a 'vice nouveau', a new sort of 'misanthropie orgueilleuse', with literary antecedents in the work of Jean-Jacques Rousseau and Goethe's *Werther* and a cultural parallel in England. While much of Chateaubriand's discourse points to his originality in creating the different figure of René, there is at the same time a desire to indicate Classical precedents and thereby an intention to generalize and say something not just about a new phenomenon, but also about what he sees as the human condition as a whole. The preface ends by underlining once again the moral purpose of the work.

(iv) *Concluding remarks*

This long examination of the prefaces to *Atala* and *René* and of the relationship of the texts to the *Génie du christianisme* makes abundantly clear, I hope, the wide range of themes and preoccupations which Chateaubriand was determined to put before his audience. Most of these concern the public interest: problems of religion and morality, of politics, of their expression by literary convention and invention. Apart, however, from the insistence on his knowledge of North America, the one element which is surprisingly absent from this material is that which is so often referred to by subsequent commentators on the works: that is, their confessional nature and the preoccupation with self. It is all the more odd, therefore, that so many modern critics should have

---

Chateaubriand's life which he is recalling, the moment at which he is writing, then later re-writing, and commentary on both periods. It is, however, a technique used from his earliest days, when he pillaged his own manuscripts or publications at different times for different purposes. The description of Niagara Falls, for example, at the end of *Atala* (p.136) had already been used in slightly different form in the *Essai sur les révolutions* and then was reworked for the *Voyage en Amérique* and the *Mémoires d'outre-tombe*. The description was probably composed originally for *Les Natchez*, his American Indian epic.

ignored or underplayed these public issues implicit in the two texts, issues made so explicit by the prefaces and the context of *Génie du christianisme*.

Above all, if you read the two narratives *in situ* in the *Génie*, it seems to me impossible to deny the seriousness of intention behind the politico-religious purpose of the work. One can argue legitimately about the exact nature of Chateaubriand's Christian convictions and about how convincing a demonstration he provides, but not about the depth of his commitment to them as fit subjects of literature. *Atala* and *René* constitute about one eighth of the full text of the *Génie* and there is no way in which the remaining seven eighths can be seen as merely the setting for the two short *récits*. The attempt to restore Christianity to its proper place, as Chateaubriand saw it, in the cultural life of France and to begin by demonstrating not only its past superiority in the field of literary inspiration but also its present creative potential was of the essence. The opening lines of the *Génie* display the battling, even polemical, intention:

> Depuis que le christianisme a paru sur la terre, trois espèces d'ennemis l'ont constamment attaqué: les hérésiarques, les sophistes, et ces hommes en apparence frivoles, qui détruisent tout en riant. De nombreux apologistes ont victorieusement répondu aux subtilités et aux mensonges; mais ils ont été moins heureux contre la dérision. (*6*, p.465)

At the very outset of the nineteenth century, then, Chateaubriand intends to combat the third group and what he sees as the mocking of religion typical of so many of the writers of the eighteenth century: to fight not so much Voltaire – for he sees certain virtues in his works – as Voltairianism or the general acceptance among educated folk that religious belief was ridiculous or even barbarous. At times he aims even higher: at nothing less than reversing the whole weight of the eighteenth-century *philosophe* spirit. Even the *Encyclopédie*, that high-water mark of the Enlightenment, is dismissed as 'cette Babel des sciences et de la raison' (*6*, p.468). One way in which Chateaubriand is determined that we shall read his two brief texts is in the context of anti-*philosophe* polemics. The paradox is that while denying the past century, Chateaubriand at one and the same time uses so many of its values and sources of inspiration, even as he is engaged in the enterprise of transforming them.

2. Texts

(i) *The overall structures*

The initial impression conveyed by the divisions of *Atala* is one of coherence, of solidity and simplicity: a brief prologue and epilogue framing a narrative. This was one of the points Chateaubriand had made in his preface to the first edition of *Atala*. Cloaking himself with the prestige of Ancient Greece he had written (p.35) 'J'ai donné à ce petit ouvrage les formes les plus antiques'. The analogy is with the early recital of Homeric epic, an oral performance of an episode framed by an introduction and what seems to be a conclusion. It is worth noting that, as Chateaubriand puts it, the early performers of Homer sang 'fragments' of the whole epic; in just such a way *Atala* may be seen as an episode, a fragment of Chateaubriand's at least partly written but as yet unpublished prose epic, *Les Natchez*. Thus, the epilogue, which in one sense Chateaubriand encourages us to see as providing a conclusion to his narrative, is at best an interim conclusion, a false closing down of the issues raised in the narrative. *Atala* is at one and the same time a whole and a part of a larger whole, a unit *and* a fragment.

The oral narrative proper, the *récit*, is divided into four sections, *les Chasseurs*, *les Laboureurs*, *le Drame* and *les Funérailles*. The titles of the first two sections once again point to a structure which appears balanced and solid, with the nomadic, tribal, hunting economy, cruel in its ways (les Chasseurs) set in contrast to the settled, detribalized, pastoral community, Christianized, gentle and harmonious (les Laboureurs). In other words certain images of 'savage' society are measured against other images of 'civilized' society. This is the overt 'subject' of the *récit*, proposed in the first paragraph of the narrative when Chactas says to René (p.73): 'Je vois en toi l'homme civilisé qui s'est fait sauvage; tu vois en moi l'homme sauvage, que le grand Esprit...a voulu civiliser...Qui, de toi ou de moi, a le plus gagné ou le plus perdu à ce changement de position?' Such a question is typical of so many eighteenth-century novels, *contes philosophiques* or *dialogues* (see pp.57-58 below). It is also the type of question which was set as competitive essay topic by French literary and scientific Academies. The topic of the 'savage' (or the natural) versus the 'civilized' is itself so common in the eighteenth century as to be almost hackneyed and certainly commonplace by 1801. We can see, therefore, that in the structure and theme of the *récit*, Chateaubriand is reflecting the literary-philosophical conditioning of his eighteenth-century background, and providing his readers with at least one frame with which they would have been familiar.

On the other hand, the amount of space accorded to the treatment of 'les chasseurs' (28 pages) outweighs considerably that granted to 'les laboureurs' (8½ pages), and this imbalance raises the question of whether Chateaubriand is more interested in the 'savage' way than the 'civilized'. One can certainly redress the balance by associating the last two sections of the *récit* with 'les laboureurs' (a further 8½ and 14½ pages, making 31½ pages in all). Such a conflation of the last three sections of the *récit* is not unreasonable as all three are situated in the little pastoral world dominated by the presence of *père* Aubry. Furthermore, the opening paragraph of the *Epilogue* picks up the precise terms of the contrast, though not of the specific question, posed at the outset of the *récit*: 'Je vis dans ce récit le tableau du peuple chasseur et du peuple laboureur...' (p.133).

This seems to give a satisfying binary structure to the *récit* (*Chasseurs/Laboureurs*), but the fact remains that the sections entitled *le Drame* and *les Funérailles* have been hived off and presented separately – they are not sub-sections of *les Laboureurs* – and this tends to undermine the initial impression I have just mentioned. It is as if the 'philosophical' debate proposed – and in a number of respects actually discussed – has slipped out of focus because of the eruption of the personal drama and its consequences for Chactas. Indeed, when one looks a little more closely, the proposed debate between the savage and the civilized is not the only or even the main focus of the *chasseur-laboureur* sections. The personal interiorized struggle of Atala and the relationship of Chactas and Atala to the natural environments they traverse are related only tangentially or else ambiguously to the *philosophe*-type debate and yet it is topics such as these which dominate these parts of the text. So, at the level of the *récit*, as at the level of the whole text, the obvious and ordered 'public' structures, those concerned with public issues of religion, are subverted by 'private' matters of emotion or 'eternal' matters focused on a variety of meditations surrounding the perception of desire and death.

Although *René* is rather less than half the length of *Atala* it follows the same overall pattern. No subdivisions or chapter-headings are indicated, but it is perfectly evident that once again we have the simple structure of prologue (pp.143-44) and epilogue (pp.169-72) framing the oral narrative or *récit* (pp.144-69).

The prologue uses very similar elements to those of the *Atala* prologue: the French colonial context in North America and the tableau of the banks of the Mississippi. René and Chactas are present in both prologues, but now we have the addition of a third figure, the *père* Souël, at the outset rather than encountered in the course of the *récit* as was *père* Aubry in *Atala*. Nevertheless, the impression gained is of a reassembling of virtually identical basic ingredients. Certainly the colonial theme is no longer used as a springboard for the overt political aim of singing the praises of French colonial expansion. On the other hand the explicit thematic opposition of the savage and the civilized, while no longer posed in the terms of an eighteenth-century debate, remains as an undercurrent in the tableau of the countryside around Fort Rosalie which presents 'le contraste des mœurs sociales et des mœurs sauvages.' More importantly, however, from the outset the personal, emotional problems of René, as opposed to the general 'philosophical' debate, are given a privileged position: 'Chactas et le missionnaire désiraient vivement connaître par quel malheur un Européen bien né avait été conduit à l'étrange résolution de s'ensevelir dans les déserts de la Louisiane' (p.143). The figure of the unfortunate victim and the resultant strangeness of conduct of the young man dominate the prologue thematically. This has repercussions on the central narrative which follows since it is that of a person in a continuing state of emotional disturbance. In the case of Chactas's tale in *Atala*, the narrator is a person who has lived through personal torments of a profound kind but has now reached 'repos' (p.70), a state of wise and virtuous tranquillity often seen by eighteenth-century writers as an important constituent element of happiness.

In spite of numerous similarities, therefore, we are in fact dealing with two narratives produced by narrators whose standpoint is radically different. As a result, when we look more closely at the texts, we see that in *Atala* the suspense, such as it is, centred on the reasons for the dramatic climax of the poisoning, is rapidly cleared up. All mystery is removed. In *René*, however, the secret of the hero's conduct is hinted at, skirted round and ultimately undeclared and indefinable.

Consequently, the function of the epilogue to the two works is different. Where Chactas has provided a tragic but comprehensible narrative (even though the personal struggle disrupts the expectations of the 'public' debate about the civilized and the savage), the epilogue opens out seemingly closed issues by the introduction of a new anonymous narrator, the 'moi, voyageur aux terres lointaines' (p.133) who informs us that he has picked up Chactas's tale from an Indian two generations later. Retrospectively, this revelation blurs or casts doubt on the relative clarity of what had seemed to be Chactas's own telling of his tale. By contrast, the epilogue of *René* is dominated by the comments of Chactas and *père* Souël which appear to function as a double closure to a narrative which from the outset seemed destined to be inconclusive and was perhaps in any case unreliable, given the nature of the narrator.

(ii) *Genre*

It is unclear to which literary genre one should ascribe *Atala* and

René. In the context of the *Génie du christianisme* they seem to function as *contes moralisés*, illustrative moral tales. In relation to *Les Natchez* they can be read as episodes or pauses within the larger epic narrative. After all, the story of Chactas and Atala or of René and Amélie bears at least as much relation to the theme of *Les Natchez* as does the episode of Dido and Aeneas to the theme of the founding of Rome in Virgil's *Aeneid*. There are elements of the eighteenth-century *conte philosophique* in the nature-civilization debate. The sentimental novel, with its recourse to emotion and *sensibilité* as criteria for judging response to an event, also to some extent provides a model. The mix of natural description, ethnography, philosophical and personal reflection render the two tales not dissimilar to the *voyage* genre as practised at the time, and notably by Chateaubriand himself with his *Voyage en Amérique*, his *Itinéraire de Paris à Jérusalem* or the briefer, less developed *Voyage en Italie*, the *Voyage à Clermont*, and the almost obligatory early nineteenth-century *Voyage au Mont Blanc*. All these genres provide a series of frameworks through which one might profitably read *René* and *Atala*.

Chateaubriand himself floats a good deal in referring to these two works, calling them at various times episodes, anecdotes, 'petites histoires', or 'romans'. All these terms are in a sense modest disclaimers on Chateaubriand's part. In using them, he can display an appropriately civilized aristocratic disdain, while nevertheless arguing in his various prefaces that they have a fundamentally serious aim. The word 'roman' needs to be taken in its eighteenth-century or early nineteenth-century sense of invented fiction, rather than its modern one of novel. One of the obstacles in the way of reading *Atala* and *René* is precisely that in designating them as novels or 'romans', one immediately thinks in terms of certain notions of characterization or narration that belong to a later stage in the development of the nineteenth-century novel. One thus imports inappropriate criteria for judging the works and, inevitably, in the light of them, finds Chateaubriand's 'romans' disappointing. Many a modern critic has damned them with faint praise on such grounds, by alluding to their inadequate psychology or awkward handling of plot. Certainly, one of the least appropriate modes of reading them is with the assumptions of the mid-nineteenth-century bourgeois 'realist' novel. More promising, to my mind, is to abandon the idea of the nineteenth-century novel, and to remind oneself of Chateaubriand's description of *Atala* as 'une sorte de poème, moitié descriptif, moitié dramatique' (p.35). The awkwardness of classification is underlined by Chateaubriand's use of the expression 'une sorte de', which is not introduced sloppily, as he underlines in a footnote. Perhaps the two works are best seen in terms of what eighteenth-century critics called 'œuvres mêlées', plural works, using an open and flexible form which permitted the introduction of all manner of material. The neutral 'ouvrages', used so commonly by Chateaubriand to describe them, will leave us with a mind disposed to seeing what types of narration he actually does foreground.

(iii) *Tableaux*

An extremely important mode of presentation used in *René* and *Atala* is that of the *tableau*. The first pages of *Atala* provide a tableau of the Mississippi (pp.67-69) and the concluding pages of the epilogue a tableau of Niagara Falls (p.136). Similarly, *René* opens with a briefer tableau of Fort Rosalie and the banks of the Mississippi (p.144) and the hero's narrative ends with the tableau of René on the seashore. In the course of the narratives other tableaux of varying length and different interest are introduced. For example, in *Atala*, the tableau of Florida by day and night (p.91), the Indian village of Sticoë (p.93), *père* Aubry's cave (p.102), the groves of death (p.105), the celebration of the Mass (p.107) and so on. In *René*, while tableaux are less generously deployed, one can point to the explicit tableau of René on the summit of Mount Etna (pp.150-51), in addition to those already mentioned.

At one level, the tableaux can be seen simply as pictures or paintings transposed into prose. The opening tableau of *René* (p.144), for example, underlines the pictorial qualities by providing, successively, a clear foreground from which the scene is to be viewed ('sous un sassafras, au bord du Meschacebé'), an indication of the nature of the light ('L'aurore se levait'), the middleground features ('à quelque distance...on apercevait'), an important focus ('sur la droite'), the background ('au fond de la perspective'), then by contrast a return to the foreground with the Mississippi framing the picture ('formait la bordure du tableau'), the whole being characterized as 'cette belle scène'.

The scene is quite clearly a painting in words. Later in the nineteenth century a poet such as Gautier attempted what he called 'transpositions d'art', trying to render in verse the impression created by a work originally in another art form, not simply describing, say, a jewel, but also trying to render the description in jewel-like form. Such experiments were further extended by Baudelaire who, in a poem like *Correspondances*, attempted to show hidden affinities between different objects perceived by different senses. While Chateaubriand in his description of Fort Rosalie is clearly not functioning at this level of sophistication, such perceptions are nevertheless there in germ. Mainly, however, he seems to have operated a naïve, unproblematical transposition from the visual to the verbal.

But what is the visual perception he is transposing here? It seems to me to be essentially that of certain notions of the picturesque current at the time, the picturesque being understood in the sense of a technical term in painting and other art forms. Chateaubriand had from early in his life been interested in aspects of the debate about the art of landscape painting. As example one might cite the literary exercise Chateaubriand dated 'Londres, 1795' entitled *Lettre sur l'art du dessin dans les paysages*,[9] in which he discusses the subject fairly superficially, calling for control of the imagination by direct study of nature and rejecting artificial notions of the sublime. Landscapes he says, however, are not idle illustrations; they belong with the study of humanity: 'Le paysage a sa partie morale et intellectuelle comme le portrait; il faut qu'il parle aussi, et qu'à travers l'exécution matérielle on éprouve ou les

---

[9] Published in *Correspondance générale*, Paris, Gallimard, 1977, Vol.I, pp.69-73.

rêveries ou les sentiments que font naître les différents sites'.[10] A good example of the non-fictional application of such a principle can be found in Chateaubriand's letter to Fontanes on the Roman *campagna*,[11] where the direct observation and presentation of scenery is intimately linked with considerations of the passing of time and mortality. Landscape description is thus to be at one and the same time realistic and ideal, natural and organized, pleasurable and morally uplifting. The latter part of the eighteenth century was a period when the picturesque mode of appreciating landscape was such that it gave an underlying coherence to arts as different as painting, poetry, prose, travel literature and landscape architecture. To the contemporary reader, one of the pleasures of reading *Atala* (and to a lesser extent *René*) was that they brought to life, by a representation in poetic prose, the 'landscape with figures' that had become a dominant manner in painting. In *Atala* in particular the figures of the two lovers wander through a succession of picturesque landscapes.

The strong presence of a prose form of the aesthetic concepts of the picturesque, however, is contrasted by what is usually seen as the quite distinct and opposed aesthetic concept of the sublime. The latter exploits certain notions of vastness, obscurity, confusion linked with terror, fear of death or desire for self-preservation, and aspiration for the Infinite. The most obvious illustration of such a concept is to be found in the storm scene in *Atala*, where all these elements are concentrated in a *fortissimo* presentation (pp.96-98). The first sounds of thunder are designated 'bruits sublimes'. The seemingly banal, some would say 'Classical' or conventional adjective, has in fact the precise purpose here of directing the reader towards the appropriate aesthetic mode for appreciating the ensuing scene. This is followed by a sequence of images of terror: fear of being sucked into swamps and clutched at by tendrils of plants, rustlings and roarings created by a whole lunatic zoo of animals,

---

[10] *Correspondance générale*, Paris, Gallimard, 1977, Vol. I., p.70.

[11] Dated 'le 10 janvier 1804'. It was subsequently incorporated in his *Voyage en Italie* (see 5, II, pp.1476-96).

reptiles and insects. The actual description of the storm is presented as a chaos of sense impressions, a sort of abyss in the sky which reverses, while retaining the same connotations, the image of the abyss in the earth which René experiences on the summit of Etna: 'le ciel s'ouvre coup sur coup et, à travers ses crevasses, on aperçoit de nouveaux cieux et des campagnes ardentes.' Now, while all this scene can well be interpreted theoretically as an imaginative correlative for the storm of emotions being experienced by the two lovers – it is the moment when Chactas is about to sweep away the last barriers of resistance put up by Atala (Chactas's discreet narrative of the sexual crisis is: 'je touchais au moment du bonheur') – it is, aesthetically speaking, a sublime picture, the pictorial effect at the height of the storm being underlined by the attention drawn to the *spectacle* and its capacity for transcribing terror and transmuting it into an aesthetically satisfying image: 'Quel affreux, quel magnifique spectacle!' Here again, what was later to become the merest conventional exclamation, reflects a precise aesthetic concept, that of the sublime. Just before the tableau is broken up by the arrival of *père* Aubry, the aesthetic mode is hammered home when the whole pictorial environment is characterized as 'affreuse et sublime nature'.

The presentation of the Niagara Falls at the end of *Atala* (p.136) also belongs to the aesthetic of the sublime. Even if at times there are brief elements from the geographical textbook ('sa hauteur perpendiculaire est de cent quarante-quatre pieds') from the outset it has emotional colouring ('d'affreux mugissements') and all the component elements of the immensity and chaos of nature, and the emotion induced by the 'spectacle' is summed up as 'un plaisir mêlé de terreur'.

It is possible, then, to read *Atala* as a sequence of picturesque and sublime paintings. While the presentation of the Niagara Falls can be seen as a distant echo of the major sublime painting of the storm, recalling the turmoil of emotion now long past, the dominant mode in the work nevertheless is that of the picturesque, with its overtones of richness, grace, harmony and pleasure. This is particularly clear in the organization of the opening tableau of *Atala*

(pp.67-69) but also, more surprisingly, in what one would expect to
be the elegiac 'bocages de la mort' tableau (pp.105-06). Once again,
the description is structured like a painting, with branchless pine
trees framing the picture, part of the perspective closed off by the
vast natural bridge, hills on both sides and a stream winding
through the landscape. The whole is a 'riant asile', the
'mugissement' here is not 'affreux' but 'sourd' and in any case
dominated by birdsong celebrating 'une fête éternelle'.[12]

The presentation of *Atala* as a linked sequence of paintings is
surely one of the reasons why this text gave rise to such an abundant
iconography, though few of the illustrations attempt to express fully
the contrasting values of the picturesque and the sublime which
Chateaubriand had so obviously incorporated, and tend instead to
pick out the moral or the sentimental.

René is less dominated by pictorial values, even if the analysis
I have sketched of part of the presentation of the setting for the
narrative (p.144) clearly belongs to the aesthetic of the picturesque.
The tableau of René on the summit of Mount Etna is much less fully
developed pictorially than most of those in *Atala*, though it does
begin with an interesting brief exercise in a specialized type of the
picturesque, that of the aerial perspective or 'vue plongeante'. In
just the same way as René is seated on the edge of the crater of the
volcano, so this tableau trembles on the borderline between the
picturesque and the sublime, and this in turn becomes an emblem
for the sort of no-man's-land which René inhabits. Similarly, the
nocturnal tableau of René sitting on his rock on the seashore before
emigrating to Louisiana is conceived less as a painting than as a site
providing a springboard for a representation of the world of
dilemma which is René's natural environment, with on the one
hand a world of limitation, calm and closure and on the other hand
a limitless horizon of the unknown, of storm and confusion.
Although René's narrative refers to this scene explicitly as a
'tableau' (p.169), we have in fact moved from the tableaux where
the pictorial is dominant to others where the moral predominates.

---

[12] The nearest equivalent painting to this scene I have come across is by
Salvator Rosa, *Grotta con cascata d'acqua* in the Pitti Gallery, Florence.

This leads us to a whole new chain of scenes in both works which, while retaining links with the pictorial are focused more on a *staged* presentation of the moral or the emotional.

This second category of tableaux essentially exploits certain theatrical techniques developed in the course of the eighteenth century, adapts them to prose narrative and uses them in the manner of the sentimental novel. These techniques form part of an approach generally referred to in French under the heading of 'sensibilité', one aim of which was to induce, by use of gesture, certain rhetorical techniques (use of stock adjectives, 'bon', 'humble', 'vieux', etc., direct appeals to listener/reader, rhetorical questions, exclamations) and the creation of a tearful environment, a reaction of sympathetic grief in the reader, who is left swimming in a warm bath of emotionalism. Many reasons have been given for the rise of the sentimental novel and the mode of 'sensibilité' and this is not the place to go into the question.[13] The end result, however, is the valorization of emotion, particularly of a lachrymose kind which, by a sort of catharsis, is aimed at producing not just pity but a positively improving sense of virtue, morality, or piety in the spectator or reader. There is no denying that, for a modern reader, it is most difficult to come to terms with this aspect of *Atala* and *René*, with their emphasis on what seems to be so often floods of self-indulgent tears. Let us look first, though, at the detail of the techniques.

These sentimental tableaux are commonly signposted in both works by the use of the word 'scène', 'tableau', 'spectacle'. Sometimes a picturesque tableau runs on to or provokes a sentimental one. For example (p.102): 'Ce fut au milieu de cette scène' – i.e. immediately following a picturesque tableau of the view from *père* Aubry's cave – 'qu'Atala raconta notre histoire...Son cœur [*père* Aubry's] parut touché, et des larmes tombèrent sur sa barbe...' Or again (p.107), in the description of *père* Aubry's

---

[13] See Janet Todd, *Sensibility. An Introduction*, Methuen, 1986, for a good introductory study in the English context. The classic French study is P.Trahard, *Les Maîtres de la sensibilité française au XVIIIe siècle*, Paris, Boivin, 1931-33, 4 vols.

village: 'Là, régnait le mélange le plus touchant de la vie sociale et
de la vie de la nature...J'errais avec ravissement au milieu de ces
tableaux...' The tableaux here are no longer 'paintings', but
emotional images of a Christian community combining the best in
traditional natural ways with a simple pastoral existence, which lead
on to a sequence of socio-political conclusions presented in terms of
morally superior attitudes.

Theatrical tableaux were developed particularly as a resource
for the 'drame bourgeois' of the eighteenth century, middle-class,
serious, morally-elevating plays many of them revolving round
family relationships. Diderot was both theoretician and practitioner
of this art form and in his *Entretiens sur le Fils naturel*, for
example, he underlines the technique and functions of the stage
tableau. A not dissimilar inspiration is clearly at the back of several
scenes in *Atala* and *René* as in the highly theatrical use of lighting,
speech, gesture and staged pause to heighten the emotional effect on
the discovery of Atala just after she has poisoned herself (pp.111-
12), or in the image of Atala praying (p.83) which belongs to a
limbo somewhere between a stage tableau and a Spanish mannerist
painting.

The 'spectacle' (p.164) of Amélie's taking the veil moves us
rather further away from the tableau as painting or as an essentially
static moment on stage and takes us into the world of tragic drama.
It remains a tableau only in the sense that, with its sense of costume,
ceremonial, dramatic gesture, exclamations and strong movement, it
is an engineered set piece conceived essentially in theatrical terms.
More central to both the pictorial and stage conventions is the
complex tableau of René on Etna (pp.150-51), not only in its
combination of the picturesque and the sublime, but also in the way
in which the 'painting' leads on to moral reflection ('rêverie',
p.151) and then, after conjuring up by way of contrast the image of
the 'happy savages', moves on to the inevitable 'attendrissement'
and tears.

The series of tableaux which belong to the world of the *drame
bourgeois* and the sentimental novel tend to call on the stereotypes
of these art forms and emphasize social status or function (hermit,

priest, father, son, brother, sister, old age, youth) rather than individual psychology, and this is another reason why importing criteria from the nineteenth-century novel and insisting on seeking individual psychological realism is an inappropriate critical approach. In analysing and comparing these works in the light of their use of tableaux, one can say that *Atala* makes much more generous use of tableaux than does *René*. In *Atala*, generally speaking, the tableaux are pictorial (be it picturesque or sublime) in the first half, until, as one might expect, with the arrival of *père* Aubry on the scene the moralizing sentimental 'stage' tableau tends to dominate. In *René*, there is less recourse to the tableau and much less of the simply picturesque. On the other hand, there is a more sophisticated blending of the various types of tableau which reflects the more complex, interiorized drama of René's 'secret'. In this respect, *René* is less derivative than *Atala*.

There remains the problem of the modern reader's response to the range of sentimental tableaux in *Atala* and *René*. My suggestion once again is to clear away notions of the novel developed later on in the nineteenth century which stressed essentially mimetic functions, with literature as a representation of physical or psychological 'reality', however problematical such a notion of 'reality' may be. Sentimental literature – and, as far as the 'moral' or 'stage' tableaux are concerned, *Atala* and *René* belong to this literature – is functioning, instead, in a world where it is the moral aim which is essential. Literature is thus not seeking to represent 'reality', but by using sentiment arranged in theatrical fashion as a trigger for moral response, actually intends to change the reader into a more virtuous being. While this may no longer accord with public taste or literary practice, sentimental tableaux are a specialized way of trying to change society for the better by literary means, and this is no ignoble aim. It is a form of committed literature. Because of this, the sequence of tableaux in *Atala* and *René* functions in lieu of 'realistic' plot or character to be found in later novels. Their coherence is not so much logical as in the quality of emotion, and hence the reader response or virtue engendered. This explains, too, why the 'plot' of both works often seems

artificially jerked along. For example, René's awkward justification
of his need to write to his sister (p.157) or the facile explanation of
how Atala freed Chactas from under the nose of his guard (p.89).
The emphasis is not so much on a 'natural' well-made plot as on
harmony and contrast of tableaux in the service of 'virtue'. Only by
sensitivity to the conventions within which Chateaubriand was
working can the modern reader see the extent to which he was
continuing or extending them, and hence produce a genuinely
appropriate response.

(iv) *The exotic*

Recourse to the exotic or 'local colour' as it is often termed has
commonly been used as a litmus test of an author's 'romanticism'.
It is often seen as using a more brilliant or passionate world set in
contrast to the unacceptable characteristics of everyday experience.
Thus, the Spain of Mérimée's *Carmen* or the Corsica of his
Colomba or the ill-defined 'East' of Hugo's *Orientales* contribute to
the classification of these authors as romantic. Chateaubriand's
Mississippi blues has allowed the same reductionist classification to
be applied to him too. Once again, though, his practice is more
complex than the traditional Classical-Romantic dichotomy allows
for.

First of all, and in keeping with the *œuvre mêlée* approach I
have underlined before, there is, in *Atala*, the straight attempt at
ethnography with its presentation of Indian habits, customs, system
of government even. In spite of Chateaubriand's visit to North
America in 1791, much of his information on these matters came
from French, English and American eighteenth-century printed
sources rather than personal observation. The critical editions of the
works give details of such borrowings: Charlevoix, *Histoire et
description générale de la Nouvelle France...* (1744), Lafitau,
Mœurs des sauvages américains... (1724), Bartram, *Travels through
North and South Carolina...* (1791), Carver, *Travels through the
interior parts of North America* (1778), Imlay, *Topographical
description of the Western Territories...* (1792), and so on. The list

is very long. Chateaubriand's use of them is entirely in keeping with the erudition of his time, which still tended to rely substantially on quoting of 'authorities' rather than on the more modern insistence on authentic fieldwork.[14] In *Atala*, we have elements of what was to be the much fuller handling of ethnographic detail in *Les Natchez*. Even so, it is surprising to see the range of information Chateaubriand has included here in such a small space: habits of Indian war parties, the treatment of prisoners, burial customs, details of vocabulary, food, drink and clothing. There is a particular proliferation of such information in the passage which begins with the song of a young warrior carrying a torch to the hut of his lover (pp.81-91).

Naturally, the selection of this ethnographic material is subject to the broader demands of the narrative. Although there is an interest in communicating strange ways, this is not knowledge for knowledge's sake, and many of the 'ethnographic' scenes focus on death, problems of mother and child or exile which belong to the preoccupations of the orphaned and exiled Chactas and, given their recurrence in *René*, to the more general preoccupations of Chateaubriand himself. Thus, as is often the case, the ethnography here tells us more about the ethnographer than about the object of his study.

A particularly clear example of this blending of the ethnographic and more general issues is found in the scene of the Indian 'parliament' (pp.84-86), in which Chateaubriand has carefully culled a good deal of information from his sources, but where the detail of the debate reflects succinctly a rhetorical exercise in suasion which turns on the attitude to be adopted to traditional ways of organizing society. While from our reading of *René*, with its irremediable sense of loss, we would assume Chateaubriand would slant the argument in favour of traditional

---

[14] The critical editions (see Bibliography) give a number of examples of how Chateaubriand conflates his sources, mingling details of Indian life from the deep South with elements specific to the Great Lakes Indians of the present Canadian-U.S. border. More modern notions of 'realism' are not the aim.

ways, here he demonstrates that tradition can actually be cruel, and offers the pragmatic counter-argument 'changeons les coutumes de nos aïeux, en ce qu'elles ont de funeste' (p.85). The expression 'coutumes (or 'mœurs') de nos aïeux' reflects the debate Chateaubriand had worried away at endlessly in his *Essai sur les révolutions*, as to the attitude to adopt towards the *ancien régime* in France. While emotionally attracted to the old order, Chateaubriand implicitly recognizes some of its shortcomings and the point of view of the 'matrone' of the text can be seen as a prefiguration of the stance Chateaubriand was to adopt himself later on as a politician during the Restoration.

The last paragraph of the debate (pp.85-86) 'Comme on voit les flots de la mer...' begins with an imitation of the extended epic simile which shows this passage's origins in the manuscript of the prose epic of *Les Natchez*, but closes with a rapid, impressionistic summary of the end of the debate and the condemnation of Chactas, which a contemporary reader might well have seen as a transposition of the confused and animated debates in the French revolutionary assemblies: 'Les intérêts se choquent, les opinions se divisent, le conseil va se dissoudre; mais enfin l'usage antique l'emporte, et je suis condamné au bûcher'.

The substantial dose of ethnographic documentation (and one could offer a similar analysis of the zoological and the botanical) provides a gloss of authenticity to the text of *Atala* and, while lacking in total verisimilitude, is nevertheless full of potential as a 'realistic' descriptive device which will be exploited by later historical novelists and then, as it were, repatriated and used by writers such as Balzac and Flaubert as a means of 'guaranteeing' their vision of French society. Chateaubriand has, in common with Bernardin de Saint-Pierre's *Paul et Virginie*, the relatively new element of broadly authentic detailed description of an exotic society and particularly its natural setting, though the latter is much less interested in social or ethnographic detail. This new concentration on detail masks to some extent the way in which Chateaubriand is nevertheless continuing the strong eighteenth-century tradition of using the foreign standpoint to criticize French or European society.

From Montesquieu's *Lettres persanes* (1721), Voltaire's *Lettres philosophiques* (1734) or several of his *contes*, to Diderot's *Supplément au voyage de Bougainville* (1772), the description of foreign societies and, later in the century, societies perceived as 'natural' enabled writers to dissect political and social morality, religious and philosophical attitudes. So it is with Chateaubriand.

A brief comparison with Diderot's *Supplément au voyage de Bougainville* is helpful in pointing up Chateaubriand's links with the eighteenth century and also the areas of divergence. Diderot uses Bougainville's account of Tahitian society as a starting point for calling into question European assumptions about religious, social and sexual behaviour. The main criterion by which conduct is judged in the debates which take place in Diderot's work is that of 'nature' and this loads the argument in favour of 'natural man' or the Tahitian against the European. For Diderot, one major distorting factor in human behaviour concerns aspects of religious practice and he cites the conduct of the Jesuits in Paraguay: 'Ces cruels Spartiates en jaquette noire en usaient avec leurs esclaves indiens, comme les Lacédémoniens avec les Ilotes; les avaient condamnés à un travail assidu, s'abreuvaient de leur sueur, ne leur avaient laissé aucun droit de propriété; les tenaient sous l'abrutissement de la superstition, en exigeaient une vénération profonde; marchaient au milieu d'eux, un fouet à la main...'[15] Now, in both *Atala* and *René* Chateaubriand tends to present untrammelled nature as a superior value (in spite of criticism of some aspects of Indian customs), and in that he has a lot in common with Diderot. His programme as a Christian apologist, however, causes him in his presentation of *père* Aubry and of Amélie's convent life to reverse all the terms of criticism of religious practice used by Diderot in the quotation above, and therein lies the break with so much of the discourse of the eighteenth-century *philosophes*. Since nature can no longer be used as a value one can cling to unambiguously (natural man is not always lacking in cruelty and Christianity is visibly a means of improving society, in *Atala* at least), then there can be no easy haven for mankind.

---

[15] Diderot, *Œuvres*, Paris, Gallimard (Pléiade), pp.968-69.

Diderot sees this problem in the *Supplément* and expounds it
brilliantly: 'Il existait un homme naturel: on a introduit au dedans
de cet homme un homme artificiel; et il s'est élevé dans la caverne
une guerre civile qui dure toute la vie. Tantôt l'homme naturel est le
plus fort; tantôt il est terrassé par l'homme moral et artificiel; et
dans l'un et l'autre cas, le triste monstre est tiraillé, tenaillé,
tourmenté, étendu sur la roue; sans cesse gémissant, sans cesse
malheureux.'[16] There could hardly be a more accurate characterization of René's dilemma than in the latter part of this quotation.
In focusing on this problem, then, Chateaubriand is trying to cope
in much more complex fashion with the nature/civilization or
natural/artificial debate which has rumbled on through the best part
of the eighteenth century.

Apart from the opening and closing pages, *René* does not deal
in exoticism in the way that *Atala* does. There is no exuberant
proliferation of a strange, new, plant and animal world. The joy of
discovery is absent. René's narrative, after all, is rooted in the old
world of Europe. His travels before he emigrates to America,
however, can be seen as a form of exoticism in both place and time.
His European journeying performs the same 'philosophical'
function as the North American exoticism in that it helps to define
his situation, even if it is unsuccessful in providing such a visibly
obvious contrast in the way that Diderot's Tahiti did vis-à-vis
contemporary France. René's travels after his childhood and
adolescence are distantly related to the Grand Tour undertaken by
the wealthy and the aristocratic to complete their education and, to
that extent, reinforce the interpretation of René as a displaced
aristocrat. René's tour is sketchily done: Classical Greece and
Rome, an anecdote from modern London, an Ossian-inspired view
of Scotland, Italian architecture and the final set-piece on Sicily and
Etna, all in three pages (pp.148-50). It is rather abstract, unreal
almost, and, while unnamed artists of all sorts are seen as providing
inspiring images for the traveller, in the end what is learnt from all
these wanderings? '...qu'avais-je appris...?' (p.150). Little, except to

---

16 Diderot, *Œuvres*, Paris, Gallimard (Pléiade), p.998.

reflect on time and a sense of incompleteness which reinforce important and permanent features of René's perception of the world and his relation to it. And the ultimate image of a 'monument de la nature' (p.150) simply throws back at him an image of himself ('l'image de son caractère et de son existence'). So here exoticism in the form of time or place provides no refuge; and its function as a standpoint from which to criticize the everyday is limited. Travel, for René, merely repeats and reinforces what he already knows. The insight into a new world of harmony and grace is absent. Significantly, the only vestige of the positive, exotic world of North America found in *Atala* is rejected from René's narrative and confined to the brief framing device of the prologue and epilogue, as if to strengthen its inaccessibility for René. The rock, in the last sentence of the work, on which he used to sit at sunset merely echoes the scene of his departure related a few pages earlier ('Je m'assieds sur un rocher', p.169), and can hardly be interpreted except as a vestigial reminder of consolatory contemplation of the exotic to be found in the New World.

One specific use in *Atala* and *René* of what is conventionally seen as the exotic is that of providing a means of reflecting on French colonial policy. While the highly structured presentation in *Atala* of the Mississippi and its natural surroundings together with the naming of Chactas as the narrator of his 'aventures' fit well with the traditional functions of a prologue, setting the scene and introducing the main figure, such a reading should not be allowed totally to occlude a preoccupation with problems of colonialism which are nearly always implicit in the 'exotic'. This subject is worth examining not only because it is commonly omitted from analyses of the works but also because it is another way of restating the civilized versus savage debate and also the role of the 'good' priest. I have already looked at some of the issues raised by the subject in connection with the preface to the first edition of *Atala* in 1801. Here, however, I would like on the basis of the actual text to extend that analysis and examine its literary exploitation.

In his early years of power, Napoleon's colonial aspirations were of major political interest to him even if they were later overshadowed by his essentially European continental role and preoccupations. The return to France of Louisiana, agreed by Spain towards the end of 1800, gave France control of the mouth of the Mississippi and, together with the acquisition of part of Portuguese Guiana and the retention of other French possessions in the Caribbean, potentially laid the foundations for a new balance of power in the Americas. It came to little, however, when Napoleon was forced by events to focus much more on Europe, and the ensuing sale in 1803 of Louisiana to the United States testified not only to his shortage of funds but also to the reining in of his overseas colonial ambitions.

Atala and *René* were thus published in that brief period when dreams of the French rivalling the British as an overseas colonial power were not only on the agenda but also seemed capable of realization. It is, therefore, not an innocent proposition to underline in the preface and in the opening words of *Atala* that 'La France possédait autrefois, dans l'Amérique septentrionale, un vast empire...' (p.67). It is indeed a highly political statement and one which fits with the dedicatory letter praising Napoleon. It is not dissimilar, either, to Chateaubriand's ideas some twenty years later, when he was Foreign Minister of France, concerning the role of France in relation to the Spanish-American colonies which he hoped to see develop as French-dominated Bourbon states. Chateaubriand is often perceived as a literary dreamer in politics; what is less often seen is that from very early in his career he was a politician in his dreams and in their literary expression.

Although *Atala* dates from the most openly pro-Napoleonic phase of Chateaubriand's career, the authorial voice in the prologue also implies qualifications to such an attitude when, in the enumeration of the geography of North America, it picks out 'le fleuve Bourbon' – not a neutral name in post-revolutionary France – and when it refers to the Mississippi flowing through the new Eden 'à laquelle les Français ont laissé le doux nom de Louisiane'. The name is sweet not merely for its euphony but for its containing the name of Louis, king of France. In this way the natural Paradise is associated with the lost paradise of the French Bourbon monarchy, nostalgia for the 'natural' life being linked implicitly with nostalgia for the 'natural' rulers of France, whose line was overthrown by the French Revolution. The presence of the colonial dream is thus bifocal, at one and the same time pro-Napoleonic and pro-*ancien régime* monarchy.

An element which qualifies the colonial dream is hinted at in the statement (p.70): 'Des querelles et des jalousies ensanglantèrent dans la suite la terre de l'hospitalité'. This remark sustains the idea that the colonizers were originally welcomed by the native population in the 'terre de l'hospitalité' while at the same time offering personal motives as the cause of the Natchez wars between the Indians and France; what it obscures is the economic, social and political problem of the relationship between colonizers and colonized. In just the same way, the missionary *père* Aubry is portrayed as the adored leader of his community of Christianized Indians while ultimately being massacred during an Indian uprising. The sentence quoted is probably best seen as a vestige from Chateaubriand's original idea for his prose epic, *Les Natchez*, part of which is devoted to the Indian struggle against colonization.

When one turns from the prologue of *Atala*, dominated by an authorial voice which the reader of the early editions must have associated with the brief period of colonial aspiration in the first years of the nineteenth-century, we see further comment on colonialism expressed by Chactas in his narrative. That narrative, however, is deemed to be taking place in 1725 or 1726 and to be recounting events which occurred in the early 1670s. Thus, the references to the Spanish presence and the meditation on the idyllic pastoral community created by *père* Aubry should in theory reflect a different set of assumptions or conditions from those which pertained in 1800. Chateaubriand, however, does not in *Atala* or *René* foreground the historicity of his narratives, in spite of the two or three signposts to dating which he offers us. Rather, the ambiguities which arise from the conflicting dates of Chactas's narrative and that of the authorial voice in the prologue result in a discreet blurring which allows the reader quite a wide margin of interpretation. We have seen that *Atala* can be read in the context of the *Génie du christianisme*, now we can read it as a by-product of Indian and colonial wars of the late seventeenth century, or again as an oblique comment on early nineteenth-century colonial ambitions and the loss of monarchy. This historically complex approach to the narrative is repeated in *René*, since we learn in the prologue to *Atala* that 'René, poussé par des passions et des malheurs' arrived in Louisiana in 1725. It is thus reasonable to assume that the 'malheurs' at least, insofar as they are socially determined, are a product of the turmoil of Regency France after the death of Louis XIV. So many other remarks in the text of *René*, as well as its date of publication, must, however, have led the contemporary reader to interpret the text as a comment on the turmoil induced in an individual by the French Revolution, rather than seeing it as a distant echo of earlier times.

René's narrative contains many indications which stress his class origins as an aristocrat and thus all the expressions related to exile, loss of roots or of sense of fixed position in society can be seen in relation to that fact. His sense of separation from the rest of the world, too, can be read in social terms as in part a play on 'monde' as universe, but also as good or polite society ('cet orageux océan du monde, dont je ne connaissais ni les ports, ni les écueils', p.148). The brilliant evocation of urban solitude (p.153), too, can be related, if one wishes to do so, to the sense of uselessness René experiences in a society so transformed (either in the Regency following the death of Louis XIV or, by implication, after the French Revolution) that he is unable to relate to it. Hence his nocturnal wanderings through the labyrinth of empty streets which drive him in on himself. The black labyrinth of Paris becomes the image of his mental universe. Amélie's urgings, too, contribute to this interpretation: 'cherchez quelque occupation. Je sais que vous riez amèrement de cette nécessité où l'on est en France de *prendre un état*' (p.160). Are not these precisely the points *émigré* aristocrats put to themselves after the French Revolution? It is true, too, that the first edition of *René* was more specific about René's social position and the René figure in *Les Natchez* is at times that of a social *révolté* rather than of a person suffering from a more abstract or metaphysical sickness. In *Les Natchez*, for example, rumours are spread in New Orleans that René is the political leader of the Natchez Indians, an anti-colonial fighter: 'Adario, Chactas même, et René surtout, étaient représentés comme les auteurs d'une conspiration permanente, comme des hommes qui...s'opposaient à l'établissement des concessionnaires'.[17] René is brought to trial and, just as Julien Sorel in *Le Rouge et le Noir* at his own trial proudly assumes the political role public rumour accuses him of adopting, so René makes a virulent anti-colonial speech denouncing the 'vil ramas d'hommes enlevés à la corruption de l'Europe, [qui] a dépouillé de ses terres une nation indépendante'. René is delighted to be unjustly condemned: 'se sentir innocent et être condamné par la loi, était, dans la nature des idées de René, une espèce de triomphe sur l'ordre social.' In the end a friend secures his release because 'René tenait à une famille puissante'. These are the buried possibilities of the René figure which have been deliberately toned down in *René* in the name of suggesting the more general existential woes of humanity. Nevertheless it is clear that both in *Atala* and in *René* the historically remote or the geographically exotic both lead back to the contemporary and to the political.

(v) *Family matters*

Each of our narratives recounts the story of a life and each has a good number of elements in common, so many indeed that on reading them in quick succession they appear to intermingle and form a sort of composite *Atala-René* story. Both Chactas and René become orphans or quasi-orphans at an early age. Chactas's father is killed in battle when Chactas is barely seventeen, his mother is mentioned briefly by him (pp.75 and 76), then again in *père* Aubry's farewell (p.131), but plays no further role in the narrative, René's mother dies in childbirth, an event which is related in particularly brutal and guilt-inducing terms ('J'ai coûté la vie à ma

---

[17] 'Concessionnaires' = Colonizers to whom 'concessions' of land were granted by the colonial power. This and the following two quotations are from *Les Natchez*, in *5*, I, pp.410, 412 and 431.

mère en venant au monde; j'ai été tiré de son sein avec le fer',
p.145) and his father expires in his arms when René is still young
('à l'entrée des voies trompeuses de la vie', p.147). Both Chactas
and René rely to some extent on substitute fathers, first Lopez and
then *père* Aubry for Chactas, and Chactas for René. Both focus on
crucial episodes of their lives which concern incestuous or quasi-
incestuous love. Amélie's love, as René recounts it, is clearly
incestuous (*21*); more obscurely put – René is not an unbiased
narrator and obfuscates his own reactions – and a constituent
element of René's 'secret' (p.157), or his 'honte' (p.144), is that he
reciprocates this love. Chactas and Atala, on the other hand, have
no blood relationship, but it is the discovery that they have been
brought up in the same household by Lopez and his sister (another
brother-sister image) that brings their love to paroxysm and the
immediate assumption of a vocabulary suggesting incest into their
relationship ('O ma sœur!... C'en était trop pour nos cœurs que cette
amitié fraternelle qui venait... joindre son amour à notre amour',
p.98). Following this discovery, Atala is designated unambiguously
as 'la fille de Lopez' (pp.107, 111); *père* Aubry, in trying to calm
the Gothic reactions of Atala and Chactas, 'courait du frère à la
sœur' (p.118).

Both narratives recount episodes where the male tends to the
recessive rather than the dominant role or else 'feminizes' his
experience. Atala takes the initiative for releasing Chactas and the
latter casts himself in the role of slave (pp.78 and 79) and in an
erotic epic-cum-Indian simile reinforces his submissive state:
'Comme un faon semble pendre aux fleurs de lianes roses, qu'il
saisit de sa langue délicate dans l'escarpement de la montagne, ainsi
je restai suspendu aux lèvres de ma bien-aimée' (p.79). The most
extraordinary transformation of Chactas's sexual perception of
himself, however, is during the storm scene when, with Atala seated
on his knees, he portrays his happiness as greater than that of 'la
nouvelle épouse qui sent pour la première fois son fruit tressaillir
dans son sein' (p.96). In his imagination he has feminized himself
and transformed his love for Atala into a maternal experience. The
various forms of feminization of the male are not uncommon in the

eighteenth-century sentimental novel and seek to express the superior moral qualities of the world of fine emotion, associated with the female, over those of reason or baser sensations, associated with the male. Here, Chateaubriand is adapting these assumptions for his own purposes, to soften the world of urgent sexual desire felt by Chactas and transcribed by the vocabulary of the storm: 'chaos ... mugissement ... gémissement ... hurlement ... bourdonnement ... et la chute répétée du tonnerre qui siffle en s'éteignant dans les eaux' (p.96), by transforming it into a conventionally pure and virtuous image of the mother's happiness on feeling her child stirring in the womb.

In *René*, the narrator is established as younger than Amélie (p.145), a significant detail in a society in which marriages were normally contracted between young women and much older men, and the erotic relationship is compounded with a mother-child bond, with René as child: 'c'était presque une mère, c'était quelque chose de plus tendre ... comme un enfant, je ne demandais qu'à être consolé ...' (p.158). Amélie writes to René that if he were to marry, his wife would become as a sister to him (p.160). Once again, there is the assumption of the sentimental novel that mothers, sisters, children are superior vehicles for virtuous emotion. The one departure from the brother-sister and mother-child erotic relationships in *René* is when Amélie calls on her brother to fulfil the function of father in the convent ceremony when she is to take the veil. Significantly, neither Amélie nor René can sustain the father-daughter pose and, in a scene of voluptuous, sacrilegious scandal, revert to their brother-sister incestuous role. It is Chateaubriand's achievement in these two narratives to have suggested the impasse which is created when the attempt is made to sustain both the demands of uncontrolled or uncontrollable desire and of piety or virtuous emotion.

Around this central brother-sister scenario in both works, a number of scenes sketch in other family functions. While the real parents are rapidly abolished, and no doubt this is the source for the re-creation of abnormal or artificial family-type bonds, the substitute fathers have a more substantial role. The normal rhetoric of religious discourse, with its insistence on 'mon fils', 'ma fille', 'mes enfants' is of course quite natural on the lips of the priest, *père* Aubry. In the context of *Atala*, however, with its focalization on family relationships, the words inevitably have an extra lay resonance which serves to underline the creation of a fantasy family with Aubry as father, particularly to Chactas. In his turn, Chactas in his various interjections in his own narrative as well as in René's refers to the latter as 'mon fils', 'mon cher fils' and is himself designated 'père' (pp.151, 152). Not only is the father-son relationship a sort of ideal or fantasy one, but insofar as the role of father implies authority the relationship is rendered less threatening by increasing the age gap between the young Chactas and *père* Aubry and young René and the aged, blind Chactas. Aubry is seventy-six years old when he encounters Atala and Chactas, Chactas seventy-three when he tells his story to René. *Père* Aubry and Chactas function then more as grandfathers, almost legendary figures, emblems of ancient wisdom. There are touching scenes in which *père* Aubry is described as 'father' of the Indian community. On the other hand, of the mass of periphrastic locutions for him, well over half emphasize old age and solitude, diminishing thereby the sexually authoritarian, male element in the 'fatherly' role, which in any case, given his priestly vows, one would not expect to be in the forefront. Nevertheless the two references to his past emotional life (p.101, 'les belles cicatrices des passions guéries' and p.120, 'moi aussi ... j'ai connu les troubles du cœur') do hint at a world of buried desire. When Aubry further explicitly defines old age as 'comme la maternité, une espèce de sacerdoce' (p.108), then the definition of the father's role becomes even more blurred, mingling as it does priesthood and motherhood. This blurring and displacement of social and sexual roles is reinforced by the incest theme.

The reader of *Atala* and of *René* receives an image of two successive generations of young incestuous passion. Indeed, *père* Aubry in his sermon on death extends the sequence back to the beginning of Biblical time, citing 'ces unions ineffables, alors que la sœur était l'épouse du frère, que l'amour et l'amitié fraternelle se confondaient dans le même cœur, et que la pureté de l'une augmentait les délices de l'autre' (p.120). Though he no doubt cites such cases out of Christian charity, even if he goes on to say that 'Toutes ces unions ont été troublées', nevertheless in the context of the narrative we are in fact presented with yet further incest models. Moreover, if North America is for the narrator of the Prologue of *Atala* 'le nouvel Eden' (p.67), then in Chactas's account *père* Aubry's reference to the world of Genesis and to Adam and Eve places Chactas and Atala in a situation in which they become the new Adam and Eve and to that extent deculpabilized. For, curiously, *père* Aubry glides over the element of original sin in the Garden of Eden story, merely saying, 'S'ils n'ont pu toutefois se maintenir dans cet état de bonheur [i.e. before the Fall], quels couples le pourront après eux?' (p.120). René too, fantasizes on the basis of the Adam and Eve story (p.156). In the full flood of his confused adolescent sexual turmoil, he wishes to be not only a new Adam, source of a new Eve, but the image of the latter is essentially narcissistic ('une femme selon mes désirs ... une Eve tirée de moi-même ... Beauté céleste, je me serais prosterné devant toi') before reaching a final stage, which consists in desire for annihilation and assimilation by the female figure ('te prenant dans mes bras, j'aurais prié l'Eternel de te donner le reste de ma vie'), an act which confuses religion, sexual climax, self love and the death wish in one great shudder.

If the brother-sister relationship is at the heart of these two narratives, it nevertheless exists in the context of unsuccessful attempts to reconstitute the ideal family. After René receives the letter from Amélie announcing her decision to become a nun, he pays a last visit to the family home. The description of the empty château, 'le toit de mes ancêtres' (p.163), is dominated by images of dislocation and abandonment. The visit turns into a vain attempt to recover the past sense of unity. All René is able to do, in an extraordinary sentence, before abandoning the ancestral home for ever, is to place side by side words signifying family relationships but, with no meaningful cement between them and no possibility of the relationships being reactivated, they merely function as a cry of despair and loss: 'A peine le fils connaît-il le père, le père le fils, le frère la sœur, la sœur le frère!' The absent figure of the ideal family group here is that of the mother, source of deep-seated guilt on René's part. René's love for his sister represents a positive, if confused, attempt to re-create a mother figure, an opportunity which is taken from him by his sister's decision.

The text of *Atala* does contain mother figures, but they are repeatedly mothers of dead children or associated with dead children or carriers of the bones of their ancestors. The image first occurs during Chactas's and Atala's nocturnal walk before they finally run away (p.82). The lovers are 'accablés par ces images d'amour et de maternité' but this is maternal love focused on death. The song the mother sings is dedicated to the innocence of childhood. Early death is the guarantee of preservation from the confusions of adolescence and the ways of the world: 'Heureux ceux qui meurent au berceau' (p.82). The image of the mother and dead child recurs in the epilogue to *Atala* where the 'real' narrator two generations later witnesses 'la fille de la fille de René' (p.137)[18] carrying out the same ritual for a dead child, who turns out to be the end of René's family line. This time, however, the song is not one of the innocence of childhood, but the loss of the future that might have been. The scenario of mother and dead child is repeated in slightly more obscure form in the reference to the story of Agar in the Book of Genesis (p.90) which Chactas has constantly in mind when he looks at Atala after their escape into the wilderness. The statuesque and rhetorical articulation of despair in *Atala* comes in substantial part from the way in which it abolishes normal family relationships except insofar as they focus on death and tombs.

The more radical despair of the *René* text no longer has

---

[18] Cf. p.135, where she is referred to as 'Fille de Céluta'. This is to be understood in general terms. Cf. *Les Natchez*, 5, I, p.575) where we learn that from René's dutiful but loveless marriage to Céluta there was a daughter named, significantly, Amélie, who in her turn had a loveless marriage and 'une fille plus malheureuse encore que sa mère ... et les derniers enfants de la nation du Soleil se vinrent perdre dans un second exil au milieu des forêts de Niagara.' This brings us to the scene described in the Epilogue to *Atala*.

recourse to recurrent picturesque 'ethnographic' support. Instead of these attempts at creating consoling images of maternity, René offers an image of himself left in a world he experiences as an absurd limbo.

René's narrative does give some weight, however, to one further family figure who has no equivalent in *Atala*, that of the elder brother. Here, sibling affection or love is totally absent and the contrast with the René-Amélie relationship could not be more complete. We do not even learn the elder brother's name. By the law of primogeniture, the latter inherits the family estate; and the image created by René, the younger brother, is of himself being cut off without a penny. (It emerges later that this is not strictly true either of René or of Amélie.) The elder brother figure assists the introduction of the inheritance theme and in general the money theme which was destined to become a dominant element in the nineteenth-century novel. Balzac's novels in particular are commonly organized around the spending or creation of wealth and its transmission by marriage or from one generation to another. While it would be absurd to begin even to try and show Chateaubriand as having anything like the Balzacian interest in money matters and their impact on family and emotional relations in general, it is nevertheless worthwhile underlining its presence in *René*, in however embryonic a form, because the concentration on 'le vague des passions' in most studies of the work simply eliminates this aspect.[19]

So it is that the inheritance law is indicated as the prime external cause for René having to leave the family home (p.147),

---

[19] In his own life Chateaubriand often enough had a very aristocratic disdain for money. However, he too, like René, was a younger son in an aristocratic family, his expectations from inheritance were small and his financial arrangements always very shaky. It is one of the quieter ironies of his existence that this figure who, in his *Mémoires d'outre-tombe* seeks by creative autobiography to construct a noble lasting image of himself which has little to do with money at all, should be revealed in the first substantial exchange of letters in his *Correspondance* to have been involved in buying and selling stockings (see Chateaubriand, *Correspondance générale*, Vol.I, pp.48-59). Chateaubriand was not unaware of the cash nexus.

and hence leads to the introduction of the theme of the wanderer, the exile, the rootless figure 'sans patrie'. The next mention of money occurs when, having taken the decision to commit suicide, René uses it as the reason for writing to Amélie (p.157). This is a transparent excuse, allowing René in fact to appeal to Amélie's emotions and secure the return to their earlier relations, and is a good example of how René as narrator arranges his narrative so as to obscure his own 'secret' passion for his sister. The fact that the excuse for writing is financial, however, is also an indication of status which is exploited on three further occasions. Amélie's letter announcing her decision to become a novice nun focuses on her motives. As a means of rendering concrete her decision, in the post-script to her letter she leaves such wealth as she has to René (p.161). The elder brother sells up the family estate and this becomes a 'rational' explanation for introducing the sequence of images of the empty and desolate château. Finally, the space in the narrative which allows René's meditations before his departure for America is created in part by the time needed to sell up the 'peu de bien qui me restait' (p.167), significantly to the elder brother. While Chateaubriand in no way develops the wealth theme, its sketchy presence provides a material underpinning to the expression of psychological states, which identifies René, his elder brother and his sister with the landed aristocracy. Precisely because of the way in which Chateaubriand underplays material factors in the text to the advantage of emotional ones, one tends to find the references to money awkwardly introduced and evidence of inadequate preparation of plot. Once again, however, we need to remind ourselves that Chateaubriand was not writing a novel on the basis of assumptions of psychological and material realism. The money theme is simply a sufficient presence for introducing or 'justifying' key elements in the work.

Independently of the elder brother's links with financial considerations, his only other function is to underline René's inability to reintegrate himself into a real family, and in particular to relate to the male line. René initially describes himself as 'Timide et contraint devant mon père' (p.145), yet he is the only one of the family to accompany his father's coffin (p.147), with Amélie listening from afar in her gothic tower and the elder brother simply not mentioned, abolished from the text. And yet it is the elder brother who not only inherits the estate but who, according to René, is the one 'que mon père bénit, parce qu'il voyait en lui son fils aîné. Pour moi, livré de bonne heure à des mains étrangères, je fus élevé loin du toit paternel' (p.145). The contrast is not simply between elder son and younger son sent out to wet-nurse, but between integration and banishment, between being blessed or damned by the father. And this is all the more important to René as, like the Indians in *Atala*, one of his strongest beliefs is in ancestor worship. To be cut off from parents and parental blessing, to find the 'toit de mes ancêtres', 'le toit paternel', empty and abandoned is a crucial family trauma for René, even if it is less visibly dramatic than the crisis in his relations with Amélie.

In both *Atala* and *René*, therefore, we have, in spite of some differences of emphasis, a set of overlapping preoccupations focusing on a simplified set of real or fantasy family relationships, mother, father, brother, sister – and some simple oppositions – youth/old age, home/exile. In both texts crucial scenes are incestuous or at least described in incestuous terms. Incest is one of the strongest taboos in Western society, deemed unnatural, abnormal, criminal. Why, then, this focusing in both these works? It seems to me that there is no simple answer to this. Much scholarly activity in the past has been devoted to discussing Chateaubriand's relations with his sister Lucile as the 'source' for the incest episodes. If there were solid grounds for believing there was such a relationship, then *Atala* and *René* could be seen as a working out in literary terms of the tensions arising from such desires and the ensuing sense of guilt. There is simply insufficient documentation to decide the matter, and so it is best left in mid-air. Another approach has been made to chase up literary models or reminiscences. Incest was not an untouched subject in eighteenth-century literature. One can again quote Diderot's *Supplément au voyage de Bougainville*, not simply for the fact that mention is made of incest, but also because it demonstrates the way in which the topic can be integrated

into a 'philosophical' discussion of the natural or unnatural and its
linkage of the individual with the social. In this work a European
priest and a Tahitian discuss incest, the Tahitian saying it is
approved in Tahiti in the name of 'le bien général et l'utilité
particulière' and, as in *Atala*, quotes the example of Adam and Eve
and their offspring as having necessarily committed incest. This
pushes the priest back on the defensive and he concedes that it may
be possible that incest is not against nature 'mais ne suffit-il pas
qu'il menace la constitution politique?'[20] This sort of discussion is
interesting and helps us to read *Atala* and *René* because, as we have
seen, one of the models Chateaubriand had in mind when
composing these works was precisely just such a 'philosophical'
discussion. The quotation from Diderot allows us to see that, in
discussing the 'natural', Chateaubriand's position is tense and
unstable, appearing both to support the 'naturalness' of incest and at
the same time multiplying vocabulary or scenes around the taboo
which state or imply a sense of guilt and criminal behaviour.

Equally, Diderot's text provides a clear expression of the
linkage between the taboo and the preservation of social order or the
upholding of the State. Breaking the taboo threatens the State. In
this context, it is possible to understand both René and Chactas as
potential disturbers of political and social order. In no sense does
either *Atala* or *René* foreground political and social questions,
though it is perfectly possible to show, as I have tried to do with the
specific examples of the Napoleonic and colonial questions, that
there is an important socio-political thread in both works. Barbéris
(*9*) has gone much further in this direction, to the extent that he
excludes most other considerations. The focusing on incest can be
seen as transposing the potential political revolt in *René* to a
different register, with the incest implying an attempt to create a
world apart from the rules of society. Its link with the Adam and
Eve myth also implies an attempt to re-create the Edenic experience
of harmony, unity and happiness before life in society shattered the
possibility of such a world. It is unsurprising and entirely consistent,
therefore, that Chateaubriand much later in his life in his *Essai sur*

---

[20] Diderot, *Œuvres*, Paris, Gallimard (Pléiade), pp.987-88.

la littérature anglaise (1838) should have given such weight to Milton, 'le poète d'Eden' as he called him, and to *Paradise Lost*, indeed publishing in 1836 a translation of the whole of the latter into French.

In *Atala* the (quasi-)incest, unlike in *René*, is not a source of secrecy or shame. Atala's secret, as opposed to René's and Amélie's, is merely the vow her mother made on her behalf that Atala would remain a virgin, by dedicating her to the Virgin Mary. It seems to me it would be difficult to discover a transposition of the political dimension in the Chactas-Atala 'incest'. Although it is possible to cross-refer to Chactas's role in *Les Natchez*, where he represents a political faction and a position vis-à-vis the crucial problem of Indian-White relations, Chateaubriand seems to have systematically eliminated all hint of this in both *Atala* and *René*. Instead, the Chactas-Atala relationship is much more closely linked by the descriptions of the luxuriant flora and fauna of North America to the Edenic and the natural. After all, Chactas left Lopez in order to go back to his 'savage' way of life. The political revolt in *Atala*, if political revolt there be, is therefore displaced and focused instead on the Utopian pastoral community of *père* Aubry. It is that environment which, thanks to Christianity, appears to have recovered both a sense of community and a sense of naturalness and harmony. It is described initially, in terms appropriate to the sentimental novel genre, as 'le mélange le plus touchant de la vie sociale et de la vie de la nature' (p.107), but modulates through a sort of primitive animistic religious world – 'j'assistais aux noces primitives de l'Homme et de la Terre' (p.107) and the priest blessing rocks, trees and springs – to the world of Genesis when 'Dieu bénit la terre inculte en la donnant en héritage à Adam' (p.108). Chactas's *attendrissement* draws the reader's attention to the moral superiority of 'ces migrations des premières familles, alors que Sem, avec ses enfants, s'avançait à travers le monde inconnu...' (p.108). This is precisely the fantasy world, the lost paradise, the Utopia in which incest was not a criminal passion and one which provides a sort of original model or justification for Chactas's and Atala's trek through the wilderness.

The incest theme, then, is best seen as at the centre of a complex of problems. At its simplest, it functions in perfectly conventional terms, as unnatural passion condemned by religious morality and, to the extent that it is indulged, giving rise to a deep sense of guilt. On the other hand, it is one of the ways in which each of the narrators in *René* and *Atala* tries to reconstitute a fantasy family from which they have been or felt themselves to be radically cut off. To the extent that incest subverts the social order, the positive excitement generated by description of incestuous relationships is a way of refusing that order and preferring an alternative mode of social organization, and this can be seen by cross-reference to *Les Natchez* to have political consequences, though these latter are not stressed in *Atala* and are only indirectly present in *René*. The strongest connotations of incest in my reading of the texts are that it is a natural passion, which not only adds the warmth of family to the passion of love but also receives religious support and justification by reference to the Biblical world of Genesis. The Edenic or Paradisiac vision is only achieved by removal or severe underplaying of the notion of the Fall and of original sin, so that incest seems to become a means of access to Paradise, a Paradise which potentially can reintegrate the physical, emotional and spiritual longings of humanity in a sort of dream of unity.

(vi) *Death and the self*

Commenting on the section of *Atala* intitled *Les Funérailles*, Sainte-Beuve wrote: 'Les funérailles d'Atala sont d'une rare beauté et d'une expression idéale ... Nous n'avons plus qu'à y assister, à suivre son convoi en le comparant à celui de Manon Lescaut. C'est bien hardi de venir rapprocher le nom de la pauvre fille de celui de la fière Atala; mais la passion, le malheur et la mort rapprochent tout.'[21] True, but the treatment of scenes of death and the way in

---

[21] In *Chateaubriand et son groupe littéraire sous l'Empire*, ed. M.Allem, Paris, Garnier, 1948, 2 vols. The quotation is from Vol. I, p.502. The study was originally published in 1861. It still has a good deal of interest.

which the theme of death in general is exploited in *Atala* and in *Manon Lescaut*, published some seventy years before, is radically different. The scene of the death and burial of Manon by her lover takes place in exile in the 'deserts' of Louisiana as does Atala's.[22] The comparison is instructive, however, mainly for the differences which emerge. First, the whole description of the death and burial of Manon is extremely brief. The death itself occupies two lines: 'Je la perdis; je reçus d'elle des marques d'amour au moment même qu'elle expirait. C'est tout ce que j'ai la force de vous apprendre de ce fatal et déplorable événement.' Secondly, although it is clear from early on in *Manon Lescaut* that the lovers are doomed to a tragic end, it is not death itself which is the focus so much as the struggle for existence and vigorous life, albeit often corrupt life, whereas in *Atala* and *René* death is an almost permanent presence, colouring a large proportion of both narratives. In *Atala* the funeral scenes sustain nearly a third of the text.

In *Atala*, after the prologue which mainly presents the magnificence of nature, within a page of beginning his narrative Chactas invokes the consolations of death as a means of avoiding or escaping from 'les malheurs qui m'attendaient sur la terre!' (p.74). A page later, he is captured and sentenced to death: ' " ... tu seras brûlé au grand village." Je repartis: "Voilà qui va bien"; et j'entonnai ma chanson de mort' (p.75). Here the 'ethnographic' detail is used in the service of the same reaction as a page earlier, that is a willing acceptance of mortality. This sentence is then exploited in a series of sentimental scenes whose sense of pity is derived from the closeness of death. We see this result first with the

---

[22] 'Déserts' and 'solitudes' are words which do not on the whole have their modern meanings in Chateaubriand's works. Both terms were commonly used by Chateaubriand in his private life as synonyms for his house in the country a few miles from Paris. In the last scene of Molière's *Le Misanthrope*, the word 'désert' seems to imply almost any habitation which is not Versailles or Paris. In *Atala* it is abundantly clear that the terms do not exclude forests and rivers, jungles even, and the presence of other human beings (mainly Indians). In other words, its use implies writing from an intensely 'civilized' standpoint.

introduction of the theme of the 'Vierge des dernières amours' whose function is to 'enchanter [la] tombe'. This produces the question which is crucial for Chateaubriand, even if it arises here in passing: 'Comment mêler la mort et la vie?' Death as a refuge is too simple a solution, because it merely suppresses one of the terms of the problem. Suicide is contemplated twice by René but rejected for the same reason. But how does one answer the more difficult question of reconciling an ardent desire for life and love, especially in young persons, with an intimate knowledge and conviction of the futility of everything, since we are all condemned to die? This is the obsessive problem which recurs in both narratives. Once this tone is established in *Atala*, then the sequence of events unravels, alternating between moments of young love (e.g. 'première promenade d'amour, pp.79-80, the young lover's[23] song, pp.81-82) and a sort of resigned recognition of the inevitability of pain and unhappiness as the lot of humanity. The latter is three times couched in the form of a 'moralizing' metaphysical apostrophe to René as listener: 'Hélas, mon cher enfant, les hommes ne peuvent déjà plus voir, qu'ils peuvent encore pleurer' (p.77) and 'Hélas! mon cher fils, la douleur touche de près au plaisir' (p.79), 'Le vent du midi, mon cher fils, perd sa chaleur en passant sur des montagnes de glace' (p.83). As part of this oscillation between desire and futility, between life and death, the 'tombeau d'un enfant' scene (p.82) arises naturally by an association of ideas in which images of death, maternity and the innocence of childhood are promoted and reconciled at the expense of suppressing images of passion ('ton cœur n'a point été exposé au souffle dévorant des hommes').

This focus on death is continued with the Indian ceremony of the 'Fête des morts' or the 'Festin des âmes' (pp.86-87). Most commentators on this ceremony underline the ethnographic interest of the scene and its sources in various 'Voyages' or studies of the

---

[23] Yet another link with *Les Natchez*. The 'Mila' in the young lover's song is the name of a young Indian girl in *Les Natchez* who is desperately, but unrequitedly, in love with René, and who subsequently is successfully courted by a young Indian, Outougamiz.

customs of the North American Indians. It seems to me, however, to gain interest from the way in which it functions as a dummy run for Atala's funeral. It appears as a way of perpetuating human emotions, of reconciling life and death, by a combination of ancestor worship associated with two specific events picked out by the narrator, one the 'baguette de saule' dance whose discreetly charged eroticism underlines the extent to which it is a sublimated sexual struggle by two virgins for possession of the 'baguette', the other the recital of an Indian 'Bible' which resembles in most respects the Book of Genesis, apart from the final episode, a sort of Orpheus and Eurydice legend which attributes victory over death to the power of song. The component elements of the day's events provide an amalgam of death, pleasure, sexuality, religion and song which, implicitly, is a form of answer to the question, 'Comment mêler la mort et la vie?' At this stage, too, one wonders whether the strange inclusion of the Orpheus-type legend, for which there is no justification in Indian religion or Chateaubriand's sources, is not a way of inscribing in the text the power of 'la chanson' (song, poetry, art) to conquer death by precisely the sort of love and death 'songs' which are provided by the narratives of both Chactas and René. The whole episode is linked, too, to one of the numerous zephyrs or breezes which blow through the narratives as if they represented the spirit of the universe.[24] The day's events end with a solemn procession to the national tomb and an elaborate ceremonial in which the bones of the ancestors are laid to rest again. The tomb theme is, here at least, a way of creating a sense of permanence and of keeping alive the memory of the dead and hence of countering the sense of meaninglessness of human existence. It is a way of giving concrete expression to the fear, so frequently articulated in the text, of permanent exile, which leads to forgetfulness on the part

---

[24] One can note how awkwardly the 'vents' are introduced by a parenthesis ('une tempête s'était élévée') as a gesture towards 'realistic' justification. Chateaubriand, however, is not really interested at all in such mimetic preparations. It is rather that his mental universe demands the presence of these vivifying winds as a compulsion. For a brilliant examination of this aspect of Chateaubriand's work, see *8*.

of others and oblivion. Hence the depth of emotion of Atala's song of exile (pp.93-94), after she and Chactas escape into the wilderness. The refrain: 'Heureux ceux qui n'ont point vu la fumée des fêtes de l'étranger, et qui ne se sont assis qu'aux festins de leurs pères!' is a way of expressing the sense of loss occurring when one is removed from the possibility of participating in the 'Fête des morts'. The meaning of 'la patrie absente' goes beyond simple loss of hearth and home, beyond an expression of Chateaubriand's sense of exile after the French Revolution, and reaches out to a universal dimension which for Chateaubriand belongs to the world of religious experience in general.

While graveyard scenes and meditations on mortality are a commonplace among Romantic writers, in the case of Chateaubriand the treatment of tomb episodes is more deeply integrated with the thematics of desire. In what amounts almost to a cult of the dead, the tomb becomes a focus for and an expression of life. In spite of its Christianization, the description of the 'Bocages de la mort' (pp.105-06) repeats many of the elements of the 'Fête des morts' episode. The cemetery is transformed into a 'riant asile', the wind in the trees provides the religious element, and the memory of the dead is perpetuated by birdsong in a 'fête éternelle'. Here nature provides the 'tomb' architecture with trees like columns in the peristyle of a temple.

It is really with the death and burial of Atala, however, that the theme reaches its full development. The delectation in, and the extension of, the thematics already sketched out, make this the climax of the work. There is the ecstatic agony of Atala, first with its frenetic expression of frustrated passion, wishing the death of God 'pourvu que serrée dans tes bras, j'eusse roulé d'abîme en abîme avec les débris de Dieu et du monde!' (p.115), counterbalanced by an expression one would expect more commonly to find in a novel by Zola than in an 'anecdote' of Christian apologetics: 'je vois avec joie ma virginité dévorer ma vie.' Then Atala succeeds in resigning herself to death, essentially by aestheticizing it and, as so often in Chateaubriand's works, by concentrating on the tomb as memorial: 'Le soleil doit être près de se coucher maintenant?

Chactas, ses rayons seront bien beaux au désert, sur ma tombe!'
(p.118). All the resources of rhetoric are brought to bear by *père*
Aubry to reduce the Gothic excess of Chactas's and Atala's first
reactions to some sort of religious balance, some notion of Classical
'mesure'. His sermon on death (pp.118-21), with its model in the
sermons of Bossuet, attempts to restore religious order to the
expressions of desire articulated by Atala's speech and Chactas's
actions which move from mere sobbing to a wild thrashing around
('Je me roulai furieux sur la terre en me tordant les bras, et en me
dévorant les mains', p.117). In the person of *père* Aubry, 'La
religion luttait seule contre l'amour, la jeunesse et la mort' (p.122).
At this stage, the religious triumphalism required by the programme
of the *Génie du christianisme* takes over as the dominant element
and ends the chapter. Its impact is singularly diminished, however,
by two facts: the minor one that Chactas confesses that by the date
of the narration, that is, some fifty years after the event, he is still
not baptized (p.125);[25] more importantly, the edifying Christian
death of Atala is succeeded by the two sections, 'Les Funérailles'
and 'L'Epilogue' which extend the emotion with a sense of
delectation. It is these two sections which reinforce yet further the
component elements we have already observed in such scenes and,
above all, provide the crucial link to the contemplation of the
narrating self. In these two segments of the work, it is not so much
Atala's death, but its effect on the living which is dominant. First,
the human being Atala is turned by Chactas into 'la statue de la
Virginité endormie' (p.128), again by a process of aestheticization
whereby the erotic presence is transformed into an art object. Then,
elaborately amplified in a sequence of tableaux, there follows the
wake, the procession to the cemetery, the burial, all this leading up
to the highly-prized state of 'rêverie' (pp.131-32) in which Chactas
meditates on 'la vanité de nos jours et la plus grande vanité de nos
projets'. This sense of desolation is slightly diminished by the
comfort derived from the way he closes his narrative with the
insistent mention of 'monument ... monument ... tombeau' (p.132),

---

[25] This unfortunate situation is rectified *in extremis* in the epilogue
(p.137).

to invoke the idea of some sort of survival. The epilogue repeats the motif of the mother with dead child, observed this time not by Chactas, but by a 'moi, voyageur aux terres lointaines' (p.133). This recurrence, two or three generations after the first appearance of this motif, reinforces the idea of ever-renewed cycles of grief of humanity. The new narrator, too, picks up the idea of the 'charme' (p.135) of the tomb, though expressing in common with other scenes in *Atala* a decided preference for the 'natural' tomb of the Indians to the pomposity of stone monuments. Thus, though exiled and without land (confiscated by 'les blancs de la Virginie', the final resurgence of the 'colonial' theme), the Indians have nevertheless saved the essential, represented by the bones of their ancestors (and of *père* Aubry, too). Life, therefore, has meaning for this wandering tribe.

The curious but important figure of the 'moi' who has heard and transmitted the story of Chactas is, however, in a more miserable position, not only exiled like the Indians, but having also lost his links with his ancestors. The last two paragraphs of the work leave the Indians with hope in 'la patrie à venir' (p.139) (however unrealistic that may be in terms of the colonial situation) but the narrator is isolated from all such expectation, left lamenting 'la terre natale' and 'la patrie'. This radical break with a sense of the past, the ambiguous use of the term 'patrie' ('the local area you came from', or 'fatherland'), must have meant, at least partly, for the first readers of *Atala* the break and exile caused by the French Revolution. The only resource for such sufferers is to turn in on themselves and cultivate their own misery: 'tu n'es quelque chose que par la tristesse de ton âme et l'éternelle mélancolie de ta pensée!' (p.139). Unless you do this, literally you do not exist or have real being.

In that sense, René's narrative takes up where the 'moi' of the epilogue of *Atala* leaves off. Hence the opening presentation of René with his 'penchant mélancolique' and his 'histoire qui se bornait, disait-il, à celle de ses pensées et de ses sentiments' (p.143). By the logic of the ending of *Atala*, René's thoughts and feelings are the only things which give him a sense of existing. Though denying the interest to others of his 'histoire' or the sense he has of self, René nevertheless presents it as more important than the 'événement' (p.143), the fact of Amélie retiring to a convent. This may to some extent be a matter of narrative strategy on René's part in order to disculpate himself from responsibility for Amélie's fate. It remains true that the struggle presented in René's narrative is between the mutual love experienced by himself and his sister on the one hand and on the other hand the attempt to construct a complete and meaningful sense of the self and its position in the universe. The latter aim is described as being attained from time to time in childhood, as for example when the parish church bell acts as trigger mechanism for the privileged state of 'rêveries enchantées' (p.146), which release an integrated image of the self, the world and time. Its components are described as 'religion, famille, patrie, et le berceau et la tombe, et le passé et l'avenir' (p.146). While in *René* the thematics of death and the tomb are not treated in tableaux as in *Atala*, nor do they receive the support of the Indian ethnographic material, nevertheless their presence is pervasive and exploited in such a way as to remove item by item the childhood sense of integration with self or the totalization of the universe experienced as self.

The death of René's father is the first occasion for meditation on the possible meaning of death (the mother's death, though traumatic, is not elaborated on) and, while offering the consoling thought of the immortality of the soul, it is accompanied by the fear that no memory of his father will remain, for memory is the means by which we have access to the past and to the continuing sense of family. Hence, no doubt, the compulsion which drove Chateaubriand in the opening book of his *Mémoires d'outre-tombe* to insist on his genealogy, not for purely aristocratic reasons, but to create the sense of participation in a continuum, the present self being, as it were, legitimized by the family tree stretching back into history. René emphasizes, however, that the very evening of his father's funeral 'l'indifférent passait sur sa tombe; hors pour sa fille et pour son fils, c'était déjà comme s'il n'avait jamais été' (p.147). The fear of being lost to human memory, this form of not-being, and hence of the meaninglessness of existence is the one that haunts René, and the one that generates the sequence of images of the abbey graveyard, the mausoleums of Greece and Rome, the marble statue of Charles II. Here the tombs and statues are not so much symbols of permanent recollection of the dead in the minds of the living as of the forgetfulness of humanity. *René*, therefore, moves beyond the tomb fixation of *Atala* and reaches out to other ways of giving meaning to the fundamental absurdity of human existence and the irreconcilables of desire and death.

One of René's strategies for coping with this situation is to focus on notions of time, and part of his narrative is deeply concerned with rendering the passing of time meaningful:[26] 'le passé et le présent sont deux statues incomplètes: l'une a été retirée toute mutilée du débris des âges; l'autre n'a pas encore reçu sa perfection de l'avenir' (p.150). He creates an image of the 'happy savage' who is unaware of such problems, since 'vous laissiez couler les jours sans les compter'. This appears as a rhetorical exercise in contrast with his own situation, as elsewhere in Indian narratives Chateaubriand produces images of the violence and instability of their society. Nevertheless, Chateaubriand's heroes, René in particular, in an attempt to simplify their problem, often create fantasies of unawareness (the desire to be a child again, or a 'happy savage', to live mechanically – 'la monotonie ... l'habitude' (p.154) – or, more radically, to be dead). Part of the grandeur or nobility of René is that, in spite of such temptations, he refuses to simplify. By narrating his 'histoire', he attempts, like the artists he quotes (pp.149-50), to give permanence to his situation. As Chateaubriand says in the *Mémoires d'outre-tombe*: 'Sans la mémoire ... notre existence se réduirait aux moments successifs d'un présent qui s'écoule sans cesse ... '[27] The difficulty, however, is in finding an adequate form of expression for such emotions

---

[26] The topic has been studied, mainly in relation to the *Mémoires d'outre-tombe*, by André Vial, *Chateaubriand et le temps perdu: devenir et conscience individuelle dans les Mémoires d'outre-tombe*, Paris, Julliard, 1963.

[27] *Mémoires d'outre-tombe*, I, 2, 3.

('comment exprimer cette foule de sensations ... on ne peut les peindre', p.155). One fleeting moment expresses the problem of the meaningless passing of time and encapsulates it in a poetic formula: when René halts on a bridge over the Seine and contemplates the sunset: 'L'astre ... semblait osciller lentement dans un fluide d'or, comme le pendule de l'horloge des siècles' (p.153). The essentially eighteenth-century conception of the universe as a supreme example of the watch-maker's art with God as watch-maker is here emptied of its purpose. It has a recognized beauty, but no longer any meaning. René's story is at one and the same time a reflection of this situation and a desperate and even, so he says, inadequate ('Notre cœur est un instrument incomplet ... ', p.155) attempt by narrative to reinfuse it with purpose, and it is for this reason that 'le chant naturel de l'homme est triste, lors même qu'il exprime le bonheur' (p.155).

At this stage, René repeats the concluding thoughts of the 'moi, voyageur aux terres lointaines' of *Atala* and claims (pp.156 and 167) that, by cultivating his 'ennui', his sense of the misery of human existence, he can begin to feel he exists. In this context, the function of the 'secret' of René, the incestuous love of René and Amélie, is merely to provide pabulum for the self to persuade it of its existence and that is why René finds 'une sorte de satisfaction inattendue dans la plénitude de [son] chagrin' (p.166). The actual object of desire has been removed, allowing René finally to concentrate on the fundamental problem. Before arriving at this stage, however, Amélie, as well as René, tries imaginatively to reconcile desire, death and permanent memorial when, in her farewell letter to her brother, she exclaims, 'Ah! si un même tombeau nous réunissait un jour!' (p.161). She, too, even at the moment of choosing the religious life, is subject to the fear of being forgotten, which stands for the idea of the emptiness or meaninglessness of existence.

As in *Atala*, the high point of *René* is centred on death and the tomb in the form of the ceremony of the taking of the veil, described initially as 'sacrifice' or 'holocauste' but ultimately presented as a ritualized funeral ceremony which leads, as in *Atala*,

to a paroxysm of physical desire in the midst of death (pp.165-66).
As in *Atala*, the Gothic blend of desire, death and religion is
succeeded by a period of reflection which extends the impact of the
scene and extracts a more intense pleasure for the self from absence
of the loved one than from her presence which, though pleasurable,
had merely obscured the savouring of the absurdity of the human
condition. Now, says René, 'je n'avais plus envie de mourir depuis
que j'étais réellement malheureux' (p.167). This is the sort of
'rêverie' condemned by *père* Souël as 'inutile' (p.170), because it is
centred on the self and not on others or on God.

        After the crisis and René's reflections complete his narrative,
the double epilogue attempts to re-establish a socially acceptable
moral order. Chactas, who has lived through similar experiences
and whose own narrative had contained more than passing
similarity to the preoccupations of René, attempts to diminish the
pleasurable anguish of the ending of René's story by covering it in a
wash of sympathy and *sensibilité* and finally by an appeal to try to
stick to simple things and live life at a lower level of intensity ('il
n'y a de bonheur que dans les voies communes', p.171). He uses the
Mississippi as a metaphor for life. While on the one hand this image
provides a satisfactory reprise of the opening scene of *René*, on the
other its detail blunts the moral point. Firstly, it implies an
infantilism which René has now outgrown as a result of his
experiences, however much he may regret the simple joys of pre-
adolescent pleasure. No more than the river, he cannot now turn
back. Secondly, because the 'moral' presentation of the Mississippi
does not 'fit' with the 'silence magnifique' and the 'inconcevable
grandeur' of its first presentation (p.144). However muddied its
waters, however desolate its banks may be after flooding, it is not
open to the mature river to become a babbling brook once again. It
can only assume fully its own nature and its place in the universe,
which is implicitly what René is at least trying to do.

        It is *père* Souël's speech (pp.170-71), however, which, in
contrast to the soothing efforts of Chactas, reintroduces a note of
harshness and a judgement of inadequacy on René. If the endings of
Atala and of René's own narrative basically convey a picture of the

nature of man's wretchedness, it is *père* Souël's function to reopen the question of a too ready acceptance of such a conclusion. At one level, his sermon is a call to social responsibility ('un jeune homme ... qui s'est soustrait aux charges de la société ... Que faites-vous ... négligeant tous vos devoirs?'). At another level, he criticizes René for that element in his narrative which has been less than a frank confession, namely his reciprocated love for Amélie. He does it by picking up the notion of shame which René had introduced in the very first sentence of his story (p.144) and subsequently ignored. *Père* Souël says: 'Mais quelle honte de ne pouvoir songer au seul malheur réel de votre vie, sans être forcé de rougir!' Basically, René had constructed for himself a pleasure in sadness, focused on self, which allowed him to keep on living, but only at the expense of ignoring Amélie's position or at best integrating Amélie's distress and sacrifice into a harmonious world picture related only to himself. (The whole paragraph 'Je ne sais comment ...', p.168, is perhaps the most concise statement of this in René's narrative.) Amélie, projected initially by René as a passionate woman (floating between the roles of sister, mother, lover), is thus transformed into an angelic, virginal martyr. A major function of *père* Souël's speech is to remind René at what expense he has created such an unstable equilibrium. It is the memory of a painfully but artificially constructed image of Amélie, with its links with desire, death and to a much lesser extent religion, which allows him to continue living, but which also, because of an ineradicable sense of guilt, provides the grain of sand which prevents him ever totally relaxing into the role of a fully integrated personality.

After this, the work seems simply to implode. Urged to fulfil his social obligations, René apparently returns to his wife, but is unable to find happiness. In any case, the reader is deliberately distanced from any possible social integration or reform on René's part, since the statement is offered as rumour only. The three figures, René, Chactas and *père* Souël are then simply eliminated in one sentence in a matter-of-fact massacre, so different from the blood-curdling effects Chateaubriand extracts from such an episode in *Les Natchez*. The last mysterious, resonating sentence ('On

montre encore un rocher où il allait s'asseoir au soleil couchant')[28]
emphasizes René's rock, repeating not only the motif of the rock on
which he meditated before leaving France for ever but also, by
association, Chactas's meditation on the tomb of Atala which is
introduced by the only occasion on which *père* Aubry receives the
curious designation 'l'homme du rocher' (p.131). These three
scenes are places of privileged meditation and insight into life and
death, movement and stability, places where the self can realize
itself in *rêverie*. The final sentence of *René* also provides for the
reader a sort of natural lay monument or memorial to the figure who
had striven to make sense of existence. The Christian programme
initially proposed is now of little import, having provided simply a
fit subject for literary works whose fundamental aim lies elsewhere.

(vii) *Concluding remarks*

One of my underlying purposes in writing this volume on *Atala* and
René has been to present the texts in such a way as to try to rescue
them from the catalogue of literary works whose interest seems to
have faded. Pierre Reboul, while demonstrating their virtues,
nevertheless felt obliged early in his introduction to the edition we
have used as our basic reference to speak of their 'grâces
desséchées', their 'attitudes figées' (pp.9-10). All works carry with
them traces of the period in which they were composed, but that in
itself is no reason for condemnation. Indeed, in looking at these
texts first in a literary-historical way and trying to convey
something of their relevance, their excitement even, to the society in
which they were written, I have attempted to show that they relate to
a concrete set of problems, political, social, literary and personal. I
hope thereby to rescue them from the curiously a-historical limbo
into which they have been thrust by their association with

---

[28] Who are these people? Where have they heard the story? Could it be
from 'la fille de la fille de Céluta' and does this sentence send us back to
the epilogue of *Atala*? Isn't this imposing too much 'logic' on the two
narratives? Isn't it rather another distancing effect to throw René's story
into some framework of the past?

generalized notions of Romanticism. That is the reason, too, why I have on the whole underplayed references to Romanticism, barely mentioned Goethe's *Werther*, hardly alluded to Ossian or *Paul et Virginie*. Although these works undoubtedly had influence on *Atala* and *René*, by harping on these Romantic or 'pre-Romantic' links I feel one detracts from the specificity of the texts under discussion.

Why, to go back to Reboul's remarks, should one describe, for example, the language of *Atala* in particular as having 'faded charms'? Why not see it, rather, as an exciting experiment in combining the structures of Classical rhetoric with various literary influences (the Bible, Homeric epic, the novel of sensibility, to name just a few) in order to produce a work which sings of adolescent desire when faced with the absurdity of the human condition, a work which struggles to show a value system exploiting feeling and naturalness to arrive at an aestheticizing of human response in the face of an otherwise intolerable situation? While *René* sheds most of the apparatus of the epic and the attempts at 'Indian' language, it, too, tells of sexual awakening, blocked emotions and the attempt to make sense of life and death. Above all, I think it is in the complexity of purpose of these apparently simple 'anecdotes' that their interest resides. They look back to the eighteenth-century *conte philosophique* while at the same time renewing it, they look forward to the personal novel, though without lumbering themselves with all the paraphernalia of psychological 'realism' which was to become such a fixed criterion for the nineteenth-century novel. Indeed, the 'cure d'amaigrissement' operated on the nineteenth-century novel by the New novelists in France in the 1950s, aimed at stripping away the realistic accretions of the so-called Balzacian novel, in many ways takes us back to Chateaubriand (though this is a point, as far as I am aware, which New novelists have never made). For these are works which do not pretend to be reflections of 'real' life, they are experimental aesthetic constructions of a new sort. They do not, in explaining, explain away problems. In the case at least of *René*, we are faced with a biased and unreliable narrator, a conscience filtering reality. We have a confession, but a partial confession. We are offered two different responses to the confession

(Chactas's and *père* Souël's), but no clear conclusion, merely an image of a rock and sunsets left to resonate in the reader's mind. This, in spite of, and in conflict with, the broader ideological context of the *Génie du christianisme*, with its commitment to Christianity.

On the nature of the Christianity proposed in the two texts, the quality or orthodoxy of the beliefs propounded, on the sincerity or otherwise of Chateaubriand's own beliefs, I doubt whether one can say a great deal that helps us to read these two texts. While the image created in *Atala* of *père* Aubry is deeply sympathetic, there is nevertheless the question of the relationship of such a mission station with the problems created by the colonial situation. But isn't the point of *père* Aubry's community that it is essentially a Utopia, a gentle, working, pastoral Eldorado? It is not a real world, and is shown at the end to have crumbled away like a dream, and so perhaps the 'real' problem of colonial relations is not an appropriate criterion to apply in appreciating its value in the text. Perhaps it is better understood, like many of the other pages of the two works, as a rhetorical exercise, an attempt to use the resources of language to persuade us of the beauty of such a community, just as elsewhere there are pages which on different occasions persuade us of the beauty or else of the savagery of Indian life. Conflating such scenes provides us with a reading which, logically speaking, is incoherent. The coherence is, rather, in the quality of emotion used to persuade. Thus it is that these two works seem both to demonstrate the superiority of Christianity and its inefficacy , both to argue for and against 'nature' and 'naturalness', both to condemn René and to approve his conduct as an appropriate response to human wretchedness. Perhaps the readings of Chateaubriand which isolate individual pages are not so very wrong after all, for a considerable proportion of both works is not only structured round tableaux but also proceeds by 'set pieces': autumn scenes, night scenes, consoling scenes, pitiful scenes; the aim being to persuade and convince us with each scene individually and successively. And this leads us to read the two texts as essays in expressing those aspects of human experience which cannot be reduced to simple coherence. While articulating a yearning for a sense of wholeness, an integration of man and nature, both texts refuse such 'simplification', except as intermittently experienced, speaking instead of lack of integration, a fragmented universe, dysfunction and disharmony. While the immediate source of such alienation is no doubt Chateaubriand's experiences in the decade following the French Revolution, he makes strenuous attempts to separate his treatment of alienation from any immediate socio-political situation, in that sense reinforcing the virtues, as he sees it, of the neo-Classical 'beau idéal'.

While the accompanying discourse of both texts (Prefaces, *Génie du christianisme*, some of the running commentary within the texts) seeks to reassure and provide a sense of order, both works in fact refuse security and order, and it seems to me that it is this refusal of simplicities which remains for the modern reader one of their most attractive features.

Select Bibliography

A. WORKS BY CHATEAUBRIAND

1. *Atala. René* (ed. P. Reboul), Paris, Garnier-Flammarion, 1964. All references in the preceding pages to *Atala* and *René* are to the 1992 printing of this edition.
2. *René* (ed. A. Weil), Geneva-Paris, Droz-Minard, 1935. The fullest critical edition.
3. *Atala* (ed. A. Weil), Paris, Corti, 1950. The fullest critical edition.
4. *Atala. René. Les Aventures du dernier Abencérage* (ed. F. Letessier), Paris, Garnier, 1962. A semi-critical edition with useful introduction and notes.
5. *Œuvres romanesques et voyages* (ed. M. Regard), Paris, Gallimard (Bibliothèque de la Pléiade), 1969, 2 vols. *Atala* and *René* are in volume I. This is the most recent critical edition of the two texts together.
6. *Essai sur les révolutions. Génie du christianisme* (ed. M. Regard), Paris, Gallimard (Bibliothèque de la Pléiade), 1978.

B. CRITICAL WORKS

7. P. Moreau, *Chateaubriand*, Paris, Hatier (Connaissance des lettres), 1956 and several re-editions. An excellent general study.
8. J.-P. Richard, *Paysage de Chateaubriand*, Paris, Seuil, 1967. A brilliant reading of recurrent motifs in Chateaubriand.
9. P. Barbéris, *René de Chateaubriand. Un nouveau roman*, Paris, Larousse (Thèmes et textes), 1973. A Marxist reading.
10. ——, *A la recherche d'une écriture: Chateaubriand*, Tours, Mame, 1974. A sustained reading of all the works of Chateaubriand.
11. G. Painter, *Chateaubriand, a biography*, London, Chatto & Windus, 1977, vol. I (1768-93). The second volume has not yet appeared.
12. C.-A. Tabart, *De 'René' aux 'Mémoires d'outre-tombe'*, Paris, Hatier (Profil d'une œuvre), 1984. A brief guide to the two texts.
13. D. Charlton, *New Images of the Natural in France: a study in European cultural history 1750-1800*, Cambridge University Press,

1984. An excellent survey of many of the factors shaping Chateaubriand's mental universe.
14. P.-H. and A. Dubé, *Bibliographie de la critique sur ... Chateaubriand 1801-1986*, Paris, Nizet, 1988.

C. PERIODICAL

15. *Societé Chateaubriand. Bulletin*. Nouvelle série, 1957- (in progress). This annual publication contains articles on Chateaubriand and reviews and bibliography of all recent publications on the life, works and related material.

D. ARTICLES

16. P. Van Tieghem, *Ossian en France*, Paris, Rieder, 1917, vol. II, pp.182-210.
17. J. Pommier, 'Chateaubriand en Amérique et le cycle de Chactas' in *Dialogues avec le passé*, Paris, Nizet, 1967, pp.57-78.
18. B. Didier, 'La Querelle du *Génie du christianisme*', *Revue d'Histoire Littéraire de la France*, 68, 6 (nov.-déc. 1968), 942-52.
19. R. Lebègue, 'Réalités et résultats du voyage de Chateaubriand en Amérique', *Revue d'Histoire Littéraire de la France*, 68, 6 (nov.-déc. 1968), 905-33.
20. D. Charlton, 'The Ambiguity of Chateaubriand's *René*', *French Studies*, XXIII, 3 (July 1969), 229-43.
21. D. Knight, 'The Readability of René's secret', *French Studies*, XXXVII, 1 (Jan. 1983), 35-46.
22. E. Gans, '*René* and the romantic model of self-centralization', *Studies in Romanticism*, 22, 3 (Fall 1983), 421-35.
23. R. Galand, 'Chateaubriand: le rocher de René', *Romanic Review*, 77, 4 (Nov. 1986), 330-42.
24. T. Logé, 'Chateaubriand et Bernardin de Saint-Pierre', *Revue d'Histoire Littéraire de la France*, 89, 5 (sept.-oct. 1989), 879-90.
25. M. Waller, 'Cherchez la femme: male malady and narrative politics in the French Romantic novel', *Publications of the Modern Language Association of America*, 104, 2 (March 1989), 141-51.
26. D. Rollo, 'The Phryné and the Muse: onanism and creativity in Chateaubriand's *Mémoires d'outre-tombe* and *René*', *Nineteenth-century French Studies*, 18, 1-2 (Fall-Winter 1989-90), 25-40.

CRITICAL GUIDES TO FRENCH TEXTS

edited by
Roger Little, Wolfgang van Emden, David Williams